Service Dog Coaching

A Guide for Pet Dog Trainers

Veronica Sanchez, M.Ed, CPDT-KA CABC

Wenatchee, Washington U.S.A.

Service Dog Coaching
A Guide for Pet Dog Trainers
Veronica Sanchez, M.Ed, CPDT-KA CABC

Dogwise Publishing
A Division of Direct Book Service, Inc.
403 South Mission Street, Wenatchee, Washington 98801
1-509-663-9115, 1-800-776-2665
www.dogwisepublishing.com / info@dogwisepublishing.com

© 2019 Cooperative Paws LLC
Graphic design: Lindsay Peternell
Cover design: Lindsay Peternell
Photos: Veronica Sanchez, Tara McLaughlin, Nancy Liebhauser, Ken Oberle

Limits of Liability and Disclaimer of Warranty:
The author and publisher shall not be liable in the event of incidental or consequential damages in connection with, or arising out of, the furnishing, performance, or use of the instructions and suggestions contained in this book.

Library of Congress Cataloging-in-Publication Data
Names: Sanchez, Veronica, 1971- author.
Title: Service dog coaching : a guide for pet dog trainers / Veronica
   Sanchez, M.Ed, CPDT-KA CABC.
Description: Wenatchee, Washington : Dogwise Publishing, [2019] | In-cludes
   index.
Identifiers: LCCN 2019002276 | ISBN 9781617812361
Subjects: LCSH: Service dogs.
Classification: LCC HV1569.6 .S26 2019 | DDC 362.4/048--dc23 LC
record available at https://lccn.loc.gov/2019002276

ISBN: 978-1617812361

Printed in the U.S.A.

What experts are saying about *Service Dog Coaching*

Veronica offers experienced R+ dog trainers a reliable business model for making a true difference in the lives of dogs and people both. The definitive read for any trainer contemplating the tremendously important work of service dog coaching.

Veronica Boutelle, author of *How to Run a Dog Business*, founder & CEO of dogbiz

Veronica's background as teacher and trainer, combined with her own experience with a disability, allowed her to develop a straightforward and practical manual which will be 'must have' for trainers who are ready to jump into the exceptionally rewarding work of coaching human and dog teams for service work

Heidi Meinzer, JD, CPDT-KSA, CNWI

As the number of owner-trained service dogs increase, this valuable reference supports professional trainers in being effective coaches of service dog clients. If you have ever considered adding service dog clients to your program, this book is required reading.

Michele Pouliot, International Guide Dog Program Assessor

Masterful, clearly-written, packed with practical information, unique, and highly recommended! Truly fills a big gap in the literature with the comprehensive information and skills that professional dog trainers need to become coaches and collaborators with owner-trainers of service dogs.

Risë VanFleet, author of *The Human Half of Dog Training* and *Animal Assisted Play Therapy*

To all of the service dogs working

to support their handlers.

Acknowledgements

I am a messy gardener. I often spill seeds and then am surprised to find plants thriving in unexpected locations many seasons later. The seeds for this book had been sitting in my mind for over a decade. However, unlike the seeds in my garden, support from many individuals was needed to make this book a reality.

Wise guidance from Gina Phairas of dogbiz prompted me to take action and move forward on writing. Pam Nashman, Kelly Spring, Tara McLaughlin and Tim McLaughlin were very gracious to take the time to review drafts of this book and give invaluable feedback. Tara also contributed beautiful photographs, as did Nancy Liebhauser. I am thankful to Larry Woodward, Jon Luke, Adrienne Hovey and the staff at Dogwise. Without Jon's interest in service dogs and his making the time to reach out to me, the seeds for this book would have continued to sit in my mind.

I am grateful for the encouragement and help I have received in my career from so many in the pet dog training and service dog training communities. My husband, Ken Oberle, also deserves my thanks. He reviewed drafts and provided support and feedback for the book. He also patiently listened to me talk about service dogs longer than anyone should.

I am especially appreciative of the service dogs in my life, including clients' dogs and my own. These wonderful dogs are the motivation for my work, and they are excellent educators as well.

Table of Contents

Introduction

When I developed a disability, I felt like the rug had been pulled out from under me. I was only 30 years old and had to discontinue my career as a school teacher. As many people do, I looked for support and information online. I had previously worked training pet dogs professionally on a part-time basis. I found myself drawn naturally to groups that focused on service dog training, given my own disability needs. I was fascinated by the cheerful, can-do attitude of people working with service dogs. I discovered that I could still use my prior knowledge and experience in professional dog training while applying my new experience with a disability. I gained additional skills in clicker training and learned that there were many ways to work around my limitations. This supportive online community included a diverse combination of professionals and dedicated amateurs. They were pioneers in the world of owner-trained service dogs. I successfully trained my rough collie to support me as a service dog and volunteered for a nonprofit service dog program that focused on working with owner-trainers.

My experience helped me gain confidence. I rediscovered a career in pet dog training, and like many trainers, I did a little bit of everything. I offered puppy training, behavior consultations and basic training, and I helped people with disabilities train their own dogs for service work. For many years the demand for service dog training was low—I received a request or two a year at most. That was probably because the benefits that service dogs could provide people with disabilities were not yet widely known. Then suddenly things started to change. I started receiving three and four requests for service dog training each week.

While networking with other pet dog trainers, I discovered that the demand for service dog training was beginning to increase dramatically for them as well. I heard time and time again from professional trainers that they were interested in service dogs, but they did not feel like they had the skills and knowledge to train them. This led me to develop *Cooperative Paws Service Dog Coach*™, a certificate program to educate professional dog trainers to train service dogs. I also started offering webinars and writing articles on service dog coaching. This book is a product of these same goals to educate pet dog trainers about service dog training. More and more, people with disabilities are choosing to train their own dogs for service work. There is a growing need for professional dog trainers to gain knowledge in service dog coaching and training, in order to help this population.

Who this book is for

This book is for the professional pet dog trainer who is interested in learning about service dog coaching and training. The training section presumes readers understand learning theory and have experience training basic skills using clicker training. The section on selecting a service dog candidate is written with the assumption that the reader has some experience conducting behavior evaluations and can interpret dog behavior and signs of stress.

If you are just beginning a career in dog training or considering entering this field, there are a variety of ways to get started. The Resources section of this book lists organizations and top-notch educational programs, books and websites for people interested in getting started in dog training and service dog training.

A note to people with disabilities training their own dogs for service work

This book was written for the professional trainer interested in learning how to offer service dog coaching. This is not a how-to book for a person interested in training their own dog for service work.

The work of a service dog is challenging. Professional support is important when selecting and training a dog for service work. An objective, experienced eye is needed to assess service dog candidates' suitability for this role.

The Resources section of this book includes many organizations that offer listings of professional pet dog trainers. Make sure the trainer you choose is committed to reward-based training methods and is knowledgeable in service dog training. Trainers who successfully completed my *Cooperative Paws Service Dog Coach* certificate program can be found online at cooperativepaws.com.

1

Why Service Dog
Coaching?

I was seated in my power wheelchair with my service dog next to me as we waited for the paratransit bus. A woman asked me, "Who are you training him for?" I was completely perplexed by her question. "He's my service dog," I responded. She looked confused, "Oh, he is not a guide dog?" Suddenly I realized, she was unaware of any other type of service dog.

When this exchange took place in 2002, service dogs were relatively uncommon. Now, there are a growing number of service dogs working with an expanding population of people with various kinds of disabilities including mobility impairments, sensory limitations, mental illnesses, autoimmune conditions, brain injuries and much more. Who knew dogs could be trained to do things like alert people with diabetes to blood sugar changes or wake up people with post-traumatic stress disorder when they have nightmares?

Traditional service dog programs

I am using the term "traditional" to describe a nonprofit organization that places trained service dogs with people with disabilities. In traditional service dog programs, volunteers begin by raising the puppies. Then, experienced professionals train the dogs to perform the complex behaviors needed and finish preparing the dogs to work in places pets are not generally allowed. The programs then place the trained service dogs with people with disabilities.

In a traditional service dog program, the organization initially owns the service dog candidate. The program has responsibility for all of the training, husbandry, food, veterinary needs and daily care of the dog. The program then transfers care and often (but not always) legal ownership of the dog to the recipient. In a traditional program, the person training the service dog candidates prior to the transfer is a skilled professional who can train much faster than a novice. For this reason, the training process is often accomplished more quickly in a service dog program than when a person with a disability trains their own dog for service work. Despite that, the process of raising the puppy, training the service dog candidate and placing the dog with a recipient may take about two years.

Service dog programs themselves are changing. They now use a wide array of approaches to train and place service dogs. Additionally, there is a range of quality among service dog programs. In the United States, the service dog industry faces many of the same challenges the pet dog training industry does, including debate about training methods. Not all service dog programs follow the same traditional approach. In fact, service dog programs vary as much in the ways they provide and train service dogs as pet dog trainers do in their work.

Owner-trainer service dog training

The term owner-trainer is used widely in the service dog industry and refers to people with disabilities who train their own dogs for service work. The number of people engaging in owner-training has increased dramatically in recent years. There are many reasons for this. When a person trains their own dog for service work, they control the process and are taking their independence into their own hands. There is tremendous empowerment in the actions of people with disabilities who choose to owner-train a service dog. Too often, people with disabilities are at the mercy of inefficient bureaucratic processes for getting needed help. A person may wait for years for a dog from a traditional service dog training program, whereas an owner-trainer can usually acquire a dog who can help more quickly.

While there are benefits to owner-training, clearly there are risks as well. The owner-trainer is almost always not an experienced dog trainer and may have difficulty doing the necessary training. Training challenges can be frustrating and occasionally even hazardous. Although owner-training is sometimes less expensive up front, if the training takes longer than expected, it can end up being costlier over the long run. More information on the owner-trainer as a client will be covered in the next chapter.

The case for service dog coaching

Service dog coaching is a rewarding opportunity to make a difference in a person's life, as well as the life of a dog. It is not uncommon for my clients to share with me how their service dogs allowed them to accomplish an essential life activity that otherwise would have been impossible. It is very rewarding for a trainer to know that their hard work has had a powerful impact on the life of an individual with a disability. By educating owners about how to select dogs appropriately for this work, and how to understand and meet their service dog's behavioral needs, trainers make a tremendous impact on the dogs. Helping owners train service dog candidates to behave appropriately in public locations has a positive impact on the community as well.

The relationship between the professional pet dog trainer and owner-trainer is also very different from the relationship between the traditional service dog program and the recipient of the service dog. The owner-trainer is hiring the pet dog trainer for service dog training guidance and support.

A professional pet dog trainer works with an owner-trainer in the same way they work with pet dog clients. The trainer offers coaching primarily via private appointments, and often group classes where the trainer is teaching and advising the owner on how to train their own service dog. Some pet dog trainers may also offer other services like board and train or day training, where they directly train the client's dog. However, these services are typically restricted to a few weeks, or a month or two at most. Rather than directly training the dog, during the majority of the training process the professional trainer is supporting the owner by providing information and education on service dog training. In short, the pet dog trainer is primarily coaching the dog's owner.

Like a traditional service dog program, when a pet dog trainer works with an owner-trainer, the service dog training process takes about two years. Unlike a traditional service dog program, the owner-trainer has full ownership of the dog and responsibility for the dog's care from the outset. The owner-trainer provides for the dog's husbandry, food, veterinary care, equipment, training and daily care needs.

Business benefits

There are many practical business benefits for pet dog trainers who offer service dog coaching to clients. Service dog work brings in long-term clients who are deeply invested in their dog's training. The training process is lengthy and can involve ongoing support throughout the dog's working career. As a result, fewer new clients are needed to fill the trainer's schedule.

Given the nature of the work, people with disabilities who choose to owner-train a service dog are usually very highly committed clients. They tend to be ready to do homework and are prepared to dedicate time and energy to train their dog. It is common for owner-trainers to seek out advanced information on dog training, read books on clicker training and even sign up for webinars and seminars that are targeted at professional dog trainers. The compliance issues that many trainers encounter with pet dog owners are typically minimal to nonexistent with this client base.

Service dog coaches have the opportunity to teach high-level training skills. No two owner-trainers have the same needs, not even if they have the same diagnosis. The customized nature of service dog training means every case is an opportunity to teach different complex behaviors. Service dog coaching is never routine.

Expanding a business to offering support for owner-trainers has the added benefit of bringing in clients interested in related training services. For example, people who would like to train an emotional support animal to behave appropriately in no-pets housing, or people who would like to train a therapy dog or facility dog, will be drawn to dog trainers who have qualifications in service dog training. Having expertise in training service dogs is also a draw for some pet owners. I have often heard pet owners say, "I want my pet dog to behave as well as a service dog."

The skill set involved in training service dogs has benefits to all areas of professional dog training. The skills required to train complex, multistep service dog tasks can be applied in everything from rally to trick training to pet dog manners.

Learning how to customize training so people with various kinds of disabilities can participate in the process helps the trainer adapt protocols for seniors and people with temporary health limitations. People with a family member with a disability will often seek out the expertise of a trainer who has demonstrated knowledge and interest in working with people with disabilities. People with disabilities who wish to train pet dogs will often seek out a service dog coach because they feel they will be better understood.

There is a tremendous demand and need for owner-trainers to have qualified, professional support in training a service dog. Owner-trainers who cannot find qualified help will often simply proceed without guidance to the detriment of themselves, their dogs and the public.

While offering service dog training is very appealing and has many benefits, service dog training is a unique and complex field. Trainers should take steps to ensure that they and their businesses are prepared. Service dogs attract attention and media coverage, which is both an advantage and a challenge. Service dog training can become very complicated very quickly. Specialized knowledge and skills are essential. By taking the time to learn the complexities, trainers grow professionally and have the satisfaction of knowing that they are providing a greatly needed service.

Bridging the gap between pet dog and service dog training

The changes in the role of the service dog and the growth in popularity of owner-training are paralleled by changes in the service dog training industry. For decades, there has been a divide between the service dog training and pet dog training worlds. Service dog trainers and pet dog trainers had separate professional conferences. It was rare for a service dog trainer to also work with pets and vice versa.

Now pet dog trainers include offering owner-training support as part of their training services. Some professional pet dog trainers also work for or even run nonprofit service dog programs.

Increasingly, service dog programs and service dog specialty trainers are taking an active role in professional industry organizations, continuing education and conferences that were previously the purview of the pet dog training industry exclusively. Pet dog trainer associations often offer webinars and seminars on service dog training. Conferences for pet dog trainers more and more include sessions on service dog training. Training programs like the *Cooperative Paws Service Dog Coach* now exist to bridge the divide between the two areas of expertise. In short, the line between the pet dog training world and service dog training world is progressively blurred.

These changes benefit both industries. The pet dog training community has a wealth of educational resources on training techniques, behavior problems, shelter and rescue dog information, and much more. Service dogs are not immune to developing behavior problems. Service dogs may come from various backgrounds, including shelters and rescue groups, and they certainly benefit from new strategies in training. The service dog community brings decades of specialty understanding of the field of service dog training, research and information on selection of service dog candidates and the benefits of human-animal interaction. This cross-pollination of ideas and information ultimately improves both the fields of pet dog training and service dog training.

2

Your Client:
The Owner-Trainer

In order to effectively support their clients, pet dog trainers offering service dog coaching need to understand some factors that are unique to this work. Owner-trainer clients have specific training goals that relate to their disabilities. There are some legal requirements as well. Some of the factors that trainers need to be aware of include:

- Disability considerations
- Cost and time factors
- Risks
- Two-person teams

Disability considerations

Necessarily, an owner-trainer must have a disability that can be helped by a service dog. The terms "disability" and "service animal" have specific legal definitions under the Americans with Disabilities Act. Many states have laws imposing penalties for misrepresenting a pet dog as a service dog. Trainers who offer service dog coaching often require prospective clients to obtain a letter from a healthcare provider indicating that the individual has a disability and needs a service dog. Communication with the healthcare provider can also be important during the training process when selecting service dog tasks. Because laws pertaining to service dogs vary by state and local jurisdiction, trainers should consult with knowledgeable attorneys to determine what paperwork is needed.

Adjusting to a disability takes time

Sometimes people will reach out to pet dog trainers for support training a service dog when their diagnosis is still very new. While a service dog may be appropriate in a few of these cases, adjusting to the limitations of a disability takes time. Rehabilitation, home modifications, learning strategies and support systems all require time, and often money as well. Adding a dog to the home when the person is still adjusting to the changes is often actually a burden. However, if the person already has a pet dog who is suitable, it may be appropriate to owner-train the dog for service work soon after a diagnosis is received. In fact, training the dog may provide a distraction during a stressful time. As always, every situation is unique.

Some owner-trainers will need help troubleshooting ways to accommodate for their disability while meeting a dog's needs. A client using a wheelchair cannot easily clean up after a puppy and may need help putting on a dog's leash. A person with a disability that causes fatigue may need support troubleshooting a dog care schedule until it is doable for them. Caregivers, pet sitters, dog walkers and dog daycare options can be considered.

An owner-trainer benefits from working through challenges and participating in the training process, as the goal is for the client and the dog to be able to work together effectively for a number of years on their own. By focusing on clients' abilities, service dog coaches can maximize clients' participation. Even people with significant limitations can often train their own dogs. I have known highly skilled trainers who had quadriplegia and severe sensory impairments. My own disability impacts my ability to walk and use my hands and arms. However, I have trained my dogs for rally competition as well as service work. Clicker training greatly minimizes the physical demands of training. A solid understanding of learning theory can go a long way to compensate for physical limitations.

Cost and time factors

In some cases, cost is the reason people choose to owner-train. The costs of acquiring a service dog from a program vary greatly. Some nonprofit programs are able to charge little to nothing for service dogs by soliciting donations. Others charge significant fees or ask applicants to fundraise. Owner-training sometimes allows for more control of expenses. Owner-trainers can decide which trainers to hire for service dog coaching, if that is the route they choose, and which training services to purchase. Owner-trainers are usually able to spread out their expenses over time by paying for group classes and private lessons as they take them, rather than needing a large sum of money all at once. On the other hand, owner-trainers assume many costs that are typically covered by service dog programs, such as purchasing specialty harnesses, vests and veterinary screenings. Owner-trainers and their dogs both vary in how quickly they learn. Some owner-trainers are able to accomplish their training goals via less expensive training options than others.

The owner-trainer who wants to acquire and train a service dog usually faces a challenging endeavor involving a significant time commitment. As previously mentioned, the start-to-finish process often takes around two years. In practice, it is not uncommon for some owner-trainers to need even more time to train their own dog for service work. Health problems, busy schedules, financial limitations and the owner's training skills all can impact the process. As a service dog coach, your flexibility, creativity and empathy will help you help your clients.

Another reason people often give when explaining their choice to owner-train is that program wait lists can be very long. It is a tough sell to tell people to apply to a program with a multiple-year wait list. On the other hand, an owner-trained service dog can be trained to perform behaviors to help at home before the training is fully completed. Additionally, for some people with disabilities, simply the pleasure of having a dog in the home sooner may be a benefit. If a person has a rapidly progressive disability, or is an aging senior, they may not have the luxury of time.

Finding a quality service dog program that meets an individual's needs is not easy. Service dog programs themselves vary widely in their approaches and training techniques. Some programs are ethical and wonderful, while others end up on the news due to questionable practices. Owner-trainers may have breed preferences, size preferences or even training method preferences that are not available through service dog programs in their area.

Risks

Working with dogs always involves some risk; however, this can be amplified if the owner has physical limitations. Adolescent and young adult dogs may be exuberant and excitable—jumping up or pulling hard on a leash can be dangerous. In your role as a service dog coach, you may need to help owners consider alternatives like board and train or day training to address some challenges. Other times, family members and caregivers may be able to help. Friends, members of the community, volunteers or apprentice trainers also may be willing and able to assist.

However, there are times when none of these options are realistic or when the risks to the individual are too high. While there are many accommodations that can help make training doable, not all people with disabilities should consider owner-training even with the help of an experienced coach. The bottom line is that for some individuals, owner-training can simply be too difficult or risky, and you may need to decline taking some clients.

Going it alone

Owner-trainers face a number of risks if they choose to work without a professional. The first challenge is that of selecting the right dog for the job. Choosing a dog for service work is a skill that requires experience and education in assessing dog behavior. Owner-trainers need to understand that dogs who initially appear to be wonderful service dog candidates may later exhibit behaviors that are inappropriate for work in public settings where pets are not allowed. Additionally, the owner-trainer may underestimate the amount of time required to train a service dog, or not be able to actually do the necessary training. Realistic expectations are essential. And while a person may be initially optimistic, it may turn out that

> they do not enjoy the process of training the dog. In that case, owner-training is clearly not the appropriate choice for that individual.

Two-person teams

Another unique challenge facing the service dog coach is when there are two human clients instead of just one. Two-person teams exist when the service dog is handled by both a caregiver and the person with a disability. Examples of two-person teams include service dogs for children with disabilities and service dogs for seniors with dementia. The caregiver facilitates the handling, training and care of the dog. For example, a parent holds the dog's leash while the child holds on to the dog's harness. There may even be more than two clients, for instance, if additional parents or other caregivers assume this role. These teams require some special considerations.

The question of maturity is important to address when working with children. Is the child mature enough to handle the dog independently, or will a caregiver be required to handle the dog? If the child's disability is invisible, a service dog makes it visible, so parents also need to consider the impact of publicly identifying the child as disabled.

In most cases, parents who need a service dog who will go with the child to school are best served by a high-quality service dog program. Dogs who are able to succeed in a school environment and work happily over a long period of time are a rare find.

Service dogs for seniors with disabilities, such as people with dementia or other neurological conditions like Parkinson's disease, are another growing area. In many ways seniors with disabilities can be an ideal population for owner-training support. They do not have years to wait for a program dog and may benefit from engaging in the process of owner-training. Also, not all seniors need or want a dog who can work in public locations, so an at-home-only service dog may be a good fit. Consideration needs to be given to caregivers as well. On the one hand, some caregivers may benefit from and enjoy training a dog. However, other caregivers may not have time, energy, financial means or a desire to participate in the training process.

Last but not least, the welfare and needs of the dog must always be considered. Service dogs are never an appropriate option if the individual with a disability or another person in the home may behave in a way that is scary, violent or abusive to the dog.

Advantages of owner-training

While there are numerous difficulties involved in owner-training, there are also some clear advantages. Owner-trainers have to commit to putting an extensive amount of personal time into working with their dog. This extra time gives the owner an opportunity to learn a complex skill set over a period of months to years. Many service dog programs have only a few weeks of face-to-face time with recipients where they provide information intensively. Owner-trainers are often well prepared to train their service dog to do additional tasks and maintain training over time. They also have the resources for supporting their ongoing training—their pet dog trainer—right in their communities.

In many cases, the very process of engaging in training their own dog for service work is empowering and can even be therapeutic for the owner-trainer. The process of identifying ways the service dog can help encourages owners to be self-aware and take control of their independence. Owner-trainers take an active role in problem-solving challenges they face from their disability. Additionally, positive training methods are themselves fun for owners to implement. The process of training the dog can be enjoyable and deepen the relationship between the owner and the dog. Meeting the dog's exercise and training needs encourages owners to be more active and participate in new activities. Isolation can be a significant problem for people with disabilities. Owner-trainers may find, as I did, that they gain social connections by attending training classes and working with their dog in different settings. Owner-trainers may even develop valued new friendships via a shared interest in the service dog training process.

Enter the service dog coach

For the owner-trainer who realizes the value of having a pet dog trainer's help along the way, the benefits can be enormous and mutual. In the best case, an owner-trainer decides to team up with a coach *before* choosing a dog. That way the owner-trainer can receive professional guidance on selecting the right dog for this rigorous work. The service dog coach can provide education, set up a training schedule and determine the best way to teach the dog the needed behaviors. The rest of the book will focus on how you, a pet dog trainer, can make that happen.

3

A Quick Look at Service Dog Laws

The information in this book is not offered or intended to serve as legal advice. Consult with an attorney for legal advice.

Perplexed by service dog laws? You aren't alone. Service dog laws in the United States are more than a little confusing. However, all professionals involved with service dogs need to take the time to understand how federal and state laws affect the training and work of service dogs.

Service dog laws have undergone intensive scrutiny in recent years. As you read this chapter, keep in mind that laws are not static, and the legislation referred to may have changed. With the expansion of the use of service animals, we are likely to continue to see increasing legislation. Service dog coaches need to stay informed about legislative changes in this rapidly expanding field.

Federal laws

There are several different laws that service dog trainers need to be aware of. First there is the Americans with Disabilities Act (ADA). This federal law defines the term "service animal" as a dog who has been trained to assist a person with a disability. Service dogs are trained to perform specific behaviors to help people with disabilities, and these behaviors are referred to as tasks. For example, the dog may pick up a dropped object for a person with a mobility impairment, alert a person who is deaf to a sound or remind a person with memory loss to take medication. The same way the ADA ensures people with disabilities can use a wheelchair in a supermarket, it protects the right of a person with a disability to benefit from their service dog's help in places the general public is allowed. Service dog trainers refer to this as public access.

People are often surprised to learn there is not more regulation of service dogs in the United States. In 2015, the Department of Justice (DOJ) published a document titled *Frequently Asked Questions about Service Animals and the ADA*, which states, "Covered entities may not require documentation, such as proof that the animal has been certified, trained, or licensed as a service animal, as a condition for entry." With service dogs there is always a balance between protecting the rights of the person with the disability and the rights of the business owner and the public. The DOJ gives some guidance to business owners as to how they can determine if the dog is a service dog. The 2010 publication, *ADA Requirements: Service Animals*, notes, "Staff may ask two questions: (1) is the dog a service animal required because of a disability, and (2) what work or task has the dog been trained to perform." An excellent resource all service dog trainers should be aware of is the ADA website, www.ada.gov. The DOJ documents referred to can be found there as well as much more information on the ADA.

Adding to the mix are the Air Carrier Access Act, Fair Housing Act and the Rehabilitation Act, which have sections that pertain to emotional support animals (ESAs) as well as service animals. ESAs are often confused with service animals. ESAs essentially provide comfort and are not trained to perform any behaviors to support a person with a disability. Like service dogs, ESAs are permitted in no-pets housing and in airplane cabins. Access of ESAs to airplane cabins has drawn particularly intensive scrutiny. In 2018, the Department of Transportation began reviewing legislation regarding access of ESAs and service dogs in air travel.

Service: not the same as therapy

Therapy dogs are often confused with service dogs. Therapy dog owners take their dogs to places they have been requested to help other people. For example, therapy dogs may be invited to a hospital to visit patients. Public access for therapy dogs is not protected by the ADA.

State and local laws

Unlike fully trained service dogs, service dogs in training are not mentioned in federal law. Trainers need to learn about the laws in their states and local jurisdictions that apply to service dogs in training. Some states also have regulations for service dog trainers. State laws may stipulate at what age service dogs in training have public access, what service dogs in training need to wear when they are in places pets are not permitted, who is responsible for potential damages and much more. Adding to the confusion, state laws can vary greatly and may use terms that are different from those used in federal law. Many states have passed laws to discourage fraudulent representation of a pet as a service animal. Counties and cities may also pass laws regarding dog trainers and service dogs in training.

The law and the service dog coaching business

While some aspects of service dog training are similar to working with pets, some of the risks and legal ins and outs are different. Pet dog trainers interested in expanding their business to offer service dog training should always consult with a qualified attorney. They should seek appropriate guidance on their business, including their paperwork, contracts, business structure and insurance. Trainers need to take steps to make sure they are protecting themselves and their clients, and following all laws.

4

Service Dog Candidate
Requirements

Helping your client select a service dog candidate may be one of your first responsibilities as a service dog coach. Being part of the selection process up front is usually ideal. However, in many cases, your client may have already selected a dog prior to contacting you. Whether you are helping a client choose a service dog candidate or evaluating a dog your client has already chosen, you need to know the qualities dogs need for this challenging work.

The ideal service dog should exhibit the following characteristics:

- Healthy, physically sound
- No history of severe behavior problems
- Appropriate age
- Appropriate size
- Friendly with all kinds of people
- Non-confrontational with dogs and other animals
- No predatory behavior
- Confident in different environments
- Easily trained
- Calm, not too excitable
- Easy to live with

Physical characteristics

All service dogs need to be healthy and physically sound. Service dog candidates should be checked for conditions that could affect their health, ability to work and life expectancy by a veterinarian. Service dogs' work is demanding, and dogs should not be expected to perform when they are in pain or have a physical limitation.

In addition to being physically sound, service dog candidates need to be the right size for the job. If a dog is being trained to provide balance or brace support, a larger dog will likely be needed. On the other hand, a medium or small dog may be more practical if the dog's primary job is to perform some type of alert. In most cases, medium to large dogs are appropriate for many types of service work. However, owners who choose giant breeds need to plan for working in public accommodations where there is limited space. Also, many giant breeds have, sadly, very short life spans. On the other end of the size spectrum, owners working with small dogs need to plan for how they will safely work with their dogs in environments like crowds.

Behavioral characteristics

There are no crystal balls when it comes to assessing a dog's behavioral suitability for service work. Service dog coaches should take safety precautions when evaluating owner-trainers' dogs. Some owner-trainers mistakenly believe that with enough training any dog can become a service dog. Dogs with a history of serious behavior problems like aggression are never appropriate candidates for public-access level service dog work. Dogs with behavior problems need calm, predictable, low-stress environments—the opposite of public access work. Adolescent dogs may fluctuate in behavior and go through periods when they are less confident. An initial evaluation that also includes a thorough behavioral history can rule out dogs who are clearly unsuited, or who have serious behavior problems. But often, dogs need to be observed and assessed over a period of time.

Service dogs will encounter all kinds of people and situations in their work. The right temperament and behavior for service work is essential. They need to be social toward all types of people and other animals as well as confident in a wide variety of situations. Service dog candidates should be considered "easy to train" and responsive to their owners even among distractions. There is no question, few dogs have the right temperament for public access service work.

Service dog candidates who are able to do public access work are a rare find and must be extremely behaviorally resilient. Service dogs may encounter children, people in uniforms, seniors and people who have unusual mannerisms. People of all ages can behave in unpredictable and strange ways around animals. People will try to distract the dog, call out or make strange noises. Although people are often instructed not to pet service dogs, the service dog will inevitably be petted by people who don't know any better or simply disregard instructions. Service dogs' behavior should always be safe, and they should never growl, snap or show aggression toward anyone.

Service dogs often work around busy crowds, in buildings, stores, public transportation and many complex settings such as on airplanes and in hospitals. They need to remain calm and focused on their work even when encountering loud noises, different surfaces and unusual sights. Dogs who worry about unfamiliar situations, objects or noises are not appropriate for service dog work. Service dogs need to be to be very confident in different environments. They need to be the types of dogs who quickly bounce back from things that would stress most dogs.

Service dog candidates also need to be non-confrontational with other animals including dogs and other domestic animals. This characteristic is more important than ever, considering the popularity of service dogs increases the likelihood a team will encounter other service dogs when working in public places. If a dog barks at the service dog, the service dog candidate should not react. The ideal service dog candidate is the dog who does not get particularly excited nor agitated by another dog's reaction. Service dogs should be safe with other animals, such as cats, and be able to perform their work even if encountering wildlife.

Spay or neuter?

Traditional service dog programs always spay or neuter their service dogs. Whether to spay or neuter is a complex and heated topic with strong opinions on both sides. Owner-trainers may make different decisions depending on their opinions and guidance from their veterinarians. If a service dog candidate will be kept intact and the dog is a female, heat cycles need to be considered in how they may impact the dog's work. If a male service dog will be kept intact, the owner must ensure that the dog does not exhibit any unwanted behaviors such as same-sex aggression or indoor marking.

Age considerations

The age of the dog is an important factor as well. Owner-trainers often approach professional dog trainers when they have young puppies, adolescents or young adult dogs. While observing a young puppy's behavior can give an experienced dog trainer quite a bit of information, behavior as dogs develop can change significantly. Because all young pups need basic training and socialization, service dog coaches can often advise owners to enroll in puppy training classes first, before assessing their pups' suitability for service work.

Even though it may take two years to train a dog to become a fully reliable service dog, most dogs should be retired by age 10. Of course, each dog is an individual. Some dogs may be able to work longer while others may need to retire earlier. Most of the time, owner-trainers approach pet dog trainers with a puppy or adolescent dog. Occasionally, clients will have an older dog they wish to train. Owners should be realistic about how much time they will actually have utilizing the dog as a service dog. It is not fair to subject a senior dog to the stresses of an intensive training process. In most cases, appropriate service dog candidates will be puppies, adolescents or young adults.

Trainability

My friend held open the door of the building, so I could maneuver my wheelchair and service dog through. At the same moment as I was exiting, a woman entered. As she passed by, she took her car keys and waved them inches in front of my service dog's nose while yelling "keys!" Phaser, my rough collie service dog, ignored her and continued walking. I could not imagine what this person was thinking, but at least my friends and I had a good laugh. To this day, sometimes for no reason at all we call out "keys!"

High trainability is an essential quality for a service dog candidate. Service dogs need to be able to be taught multistep behaviors. Ideal service dog candidates are easy to motivate, respond well to food rewards and happily engage in training sessions for a relatively long period of time. Service dogs need to tune in to their owners even in very distracting situations.

While the energy level of service dog candidates may vary to match the individual owner's needs, service dog candidates should not be dogs who get aroused too easily. Whether it is a skateboard whizzing past or children playing ball, the possible exciting distractions that a service dog can encounter while working are endless. A dog who is intensely driven to chase things that move quickly, does not calm down after getting excited or is hard to refocus around distractions is not appropriate for this work.

In a perfect world, a professional service dog coach is consulted before the client chooses a dog to train for service work. Phone or web conferencing consultations can be offered to provide guidance to those who need support selecting a suitable candidate. However, in the real world, pet dog trainers will more often find themselves approached by owner-trainers who already have the dog they wish to train for service work.

The perfect service dog candidate is very rare. Public safety always needs to be a consideration, as well as the dog's happiness and the owner's welfare. In most cases, even if the dog is a good candidate for service work, there are some minor behavior challenges that need to be addressed. Excitability and lack of confidence in different environments are common behaviors that are sometimes able to be addressed through training. Some dogs who are unsuited for public-access level service work may still help their owners as at-home-only service dogs.

Unique characteristics for unique jobs

In many ways each type of service dog is its own specialty. While all service dogs need to meet some essential, basic criteria, different characteristics are needed for different owners and different types of work. Service dog coaches are not in the same position that trainers in service dog programs are in when it comes to selection. Most of the time the owner-trainer will either already have a particular dog in mind or will have significantly narrowed the scope of dogs with preferences for a type of dog they prefer to live with.

Additionally, generalizations about a specific characteristic needed for a type of service dog may not apply to a particular owner. For instance, usually mobility dogs need to be low energy. However, a young, athletic owner who uses a wheelchair may actually need an active dog. Some owner-trainers may need a dog who can perform more than one service dog role, such as mobility and hearing work.

Ideally, the service dog candidate has a natural propensity to do the most important task needed. For instance, a hearing dog should be a dog who tends to naturally notice but not startle from sounds. A mobility dog should be a dog who enjoys retrieving. Dogs can be trained to alert and to retrieve even if they do not naturally engage in these behaviors, but it is easier if the dog naturally offers the behavior. Dogs working with children or the elderly should be dogs who enjoy working with these age groups. Dogs working with people who have disabilities that affect their emotions or behavior need to be confident and happy dogs who are not stressed by their owner's emotions or actions.

Dog behavior is not always predictable, and safety is always a priority. Some dogs may react with aggression, fear or anxiety to disabilities that cause unpredictable movements, sounds, behavior or seizures. Owners may be unaware that this is even a possibility. Owner education and careful selection of dogs is essential.

If the wrong dog was chosen

The dog was hiding behind the owner's chair in my office. I took a deep breath and began to explain, "Service dogs need to be able to walk in crowded places like supermarkets. They have to spend long periods of time in busy environments where they are surrounded by people they do not know." The owner glanced at the dog as I continued, "Your dog would be really scared and overwhelmed in a supermarket."

Selecting the right dog is not a perfect science, even if done by a professional. Most pet dog trainers have a lot of experience delivering bad news gently, and you may find that you need to do it to a heartbroken owner in your role as a service dog coach. Consider the process of educating pet owners who have a dog who is very fearful toward other dogs. Dog park visits are not appropriate for their dog. Owners need to understand what the dog's needs are, and how and why dog parks are difficult for their dog. They need to learn what realistically can and cannot be changed with training. The owners also need to learn about alternative exercise and play opportunities. Pet dog trainers often use a variety of techniques including analogies to help owners understand how their dog feels. Education on dog body language is also very helpful, so owners can better identify their dog's emotions in different situations.

Like pet owners, owner-trainers need education. They may misinterpret their dog's behavior and may not understand potential stressors. They also often do not understand what is involved in training a service dog. When this information is presented in an empathetic and informative way, owner-trainers are usually very receptive. I often use the analogy of choosing a job. Most adults can imagine how stressful it would be to be employed in a job that was not a good fit. It is important for the trainer to be empathic and acknowledge the owner's disappointment. In her wonderful book, *The Human Half of Dog Training: Collaborating with Clients to Get Results*, Dr. Risë VanFleet discusses empathic listening that, among other techniques, can help pet dog trainers communicate effectively with their clients.

Although these conversations can be challenging, they are valuable and important. Dogs inappropriately selected for service dog work typically have a poor quality of life and may develop serious behavior problems. They may even pose safety risks to the owner and the public.

5

Service Dog Training
Overview

Experienced pet dog trainers wishing to offer service dog coaching may already have many of the technical training skills necessary. However, trainers need to understand the various distinctive aspects involved in training a service dog. In this chapter, I will provide an overview of the service dog training process. Task training involves teaching a service dog in training behaviors to assist a person with a disability. Public access training involves teaching a service dog in training to exhibit appropriate behavior in settings where pets are not permitted. More information on selecting a dog, task training and public access training are discussed in greater detail later in this book.

The service dog training process is rigorous and includes basic training, task training, public access training and ongoing practice to ensure the dog's training is maintained until the dog is retired. Assessments are an integral part of the service dog training process, beginning with evaluations to select the service dog candidate. Observations and evaluations are incorporated through the task training process and during public access training to make sure your client and the service dog are ready to work in places of public accommodation appropriately and safely.

Service dogs may work for multiple hours a day, many days a week. By the nature of their work, they are subjected to training tools and techniques for much longer than a pet dog. Moreover, service dogs need to ignore distractions, focus on their handlers and be calm in complex settings. The high demands of the job are stressful for the dog.

Non-aversive methods that involve marking behavior with a clicker or another sound and rewarding desired behavior with food are effective and efficient ways to train service dog candidates. Luring, shaping and capturing are commonly used reward-based training techniques that can be used to train service dog tasks and public access skills efficiently. A service dog who learns that certain behaviors will be rewarded is, of course, more likely to repeat those behaviors.

Because many service dog skills may need to be trained precisely, training techniques are important. Clicker training allows the trainer to mark a behavior with great precision. If a dog is helping a person remove a jacket, the dog must apply a very controlled amount of tension when pulling the sleeve. If the dog pulls too hard, the dog could rip the jacket or even injure the person. If the dog is too gentle, the jacket will not come off. Clickers can allow the trainer to precisely mark when the dog pulls with the perfect amount of force needed.

By contrast, training that involves the use of aversive tools—like choke chains, electronic or shock collars, and prong collars—increases a dog's stress, may physically injure the dog, and may trigger unwanted or even unsafe behavior. The work of a service dog is already difficult without the use of a training tool or technique that causes pain or fear. In addition, training methods that involve administering corrections are very difficult, whether one has a disability or not. Excellent timing is required for training using aversive tools such as an electronic collar. Good timing is difficult for most pet owners and may be impossible for some people with disabilities. Anyone with a condition that affects fine motor control, cognition, fatigue or senses will have difficulty with timing. The behavioral consequences of any correction, especially a poorly timed electronic collar correction, can be serious. The dog experiences stress, fear, anxiety and pain, and may even develop behavior problems. A poorly timed reward on the other hand simply means the dog gets an extra treat, and it might take a bit longer for the owner to reach their training goal. A correction can also be painful for the client to administer. For people with some medical conditions, such as mine, generalized dystonia, the action of delivering a leash correction could cause pain. Disorders that impact joints or muscles may be exacerbated by the movement of delivering a collar correction. In some cases, it may be difficult or even impossible for the person to issue a collar correction.

Positive training helps build a partnership

The relationship between the service dog and their person is referred to as a partnership, and the service dog and the person are referred to as a team. Training methods and tools used should reflect this perspective and show respect for the dog's experiences during training and overall quality of life. Under no circumstance should an electronic collar, prong collar, choke chain or any other piece of equipment that may hurt or frighten the dog ever be used. During the training process, the owner and service dog will not just be honing their skills but developing their relationship. By using rewards and considering the dog's needs, the training process can be enjoyable and effective for both the owner and the dog. The dog learns that working with the owner is pleasant and fun.

The dog's emotional state and experience need to be considered throughout the training process. Training sessions should be brief and enjoyable for the owner and the service dog in training. Owners need to learn both how to teach behaviors, and also how to interpret their dog's body language and stress, so they can identify when their dog needs a break and how to help their dog through difficult challenges in complex settings.

Dogs should not be forced to endure stressful situations or environments. Locations for training should be selected with care for the individual dog's needs, readiness and confidence level. Ongoing assessment of the dog's emotional state needs to be part of each training session. Service dog candidates are learning through every training experience about what it is like to live and work as a service dog.

Working with puppies

Service dog puppies have the same needs that all puppies have, including appropriate socialization and foundation training. Traditional programs that place working service dogs with people with disabilities often have volunteer puppy raisers who have the critical role of socializing and providing basic training to puppies. Those basic training skills should already be in place before training the tasks needed for service work. Training the more advanced skills normally begins at about age 1; however, there are times when owner-trainers may benefit from having their dogs' help at home sooner. It may be appropriate and even preferable to train some tasks earlier depending on your clients' needs.

Owner-trainers working with puppies need support and coaching in providing their puppy with appropriate early experiences. This part of the training process is not very different from the support pet puppy owners need. Owner-trainers need to learn how to teach their pups basic cues such as attention to their name and to come when called. New service dog candidate puppy owners need guidance in addressing mouthing, handling, house training and crating, and helping their puppy accept husbandry, grooming and veterinary procedures calmly. Service dog candidate puppies need to be exposed to a wide variety of people, flooring surfaces, traffic, sounds and other dogs. Locations that are often good bets for the service dog candidate puppy include pet-friendly banks, garden centers, hardware stores and shopping center sidewalks. Socialization checklists and training programs that help owners make sure they are appropriately socializing their dogs, like dogbiz's *Puppy Curriculum*, can be terrific tools for owner-trainers with puppies.

Service dog puppy-raising mythology

The internet is full of misinformation. Owner-trainers may have read unusual recommendations that lead them to believe service dog puppies have needs that are very different from pet puppies. The most common misconception I have seen is that service dog candidate puppies should behave or be treated like adult service dogs. For example, some owner-trainers may think they need to put vests on very young puppies and take them absolutely everywhere, as though they were already fully working service dogs. Others may think they should prevent their puppy from interacting with unfamiliar people or dogs.

Owner-trainers may need to be reminded that puppies need time to mature, and all puppies need appropriate play, downtime, sleep and socialization. Socialization must be based on the puppy's individual needs, and activities should be appropriate, not overwhelming or scary to the puppy.

Sometimes it is very clear right away that the puppy an owner hopes will become a service dog is completely unsuited for the job, for example a young puppy exhibiting severe fear or aggressive behavior. Fortunately, most puppies do not show signs of severe behavior problems. It is, sadly, impossible to know with certainty that a puppy showing no obvious red flags *will* be appropriate for service work. Owners need to be gently reminded that the same way a parent cannot predict a toddler's future career, one cannot predict the career of a young puppy. Puppies need time to mature before they can be evaluated for suitability for service work.

Basic manners training

Between the ages of about 6 and 18 months, service dog candidates need to learn solid manners. Ideally, the basic cues have been introduced already via high-quality puppy training. This is also a time where foundation behaviors that are helpful for teaching future service dog tasks and default behaviors are introduced.

Fundamentally, the training process continues to remain fairly similar to how trainers work with pet dogs in this age group. Ongoing positive experiences in different pet-friendly locations are still important. Confidence-building activities and play are essential as well.

There are a few small differences in basic training for service dogs versus that for pet dogs. Jumping up on people and on counters is typically discouraged for pet dogs. For a service dog, it may be necessary for the dog to jump on the owner or even jump on counters. Management, such as leashes and gates, can be used to prevent the unwanted behavior from occurring without risking punishing a behavior that may later be needed. Another option is to teach and reward behaviors that are incompatible with the unwanted behavior. For example, the owner can prevent counter surfing by teaching the dog to stay on a mat when the owner is cooking. Owners of service dog candidates, like pet owners, need education on non-aversive ways to prevent unwanted behavior.

Another time that there may be a difference in training a service dog candidate versus a pet is when training long-duration behaviors, such as the Stay, to service dog candidates who will need to offer alert behaviors. Dogs who will be trained to alert, such as hearing alert dogs, need to be ready to break a Stay to perform an alert if needed. This is yet another reason positive training is so important for service dogs. Dogs who are trained through reward-based methods are not afraid of disregarding a cue.

Defaults are behaviors the dog offers independently when nothing else is cued. Service dogs are often in standby mode waiting until a task is needed. Many handlers prefer the dog to lie down quietly as a default behavior. Rewarding the dog intermittently for offering a long Down-Stay can help build this behavior. The dog can be taught to lie down on a mat initially if desired. Service dogs also need to check in with their owners. Checking-in behavior can be introduced early during basic training by marking and rewarding every so often when the dog glances at the owner.

Behavior chains

As described in Chapter 3, tasks are those specific behaviors that a service dog is trained to do to help their partner. Examples of tasks include: alerting a person who is deaf to a door knock, opening a door for a person with a mobility impairment, reminding a person to take medication or retrieving an emergency phone. Many service dog tasks are actually behavior chains or sequences of behaviors. Consider the behaviors involved in opening a door. The dog needs to grab a tether that is secured to a door knob. Then the dog needs to hold the tether, pull the tether so the door opens and release the tether on cue.

From a dog training perspective, training that involves behavior chains is both enjoyable and challenging. It is an opportunity to use those high-level training skills to elicit a complex behavior. Did you see a new training technique at a conference you just attended? Here may be a chance to try it out.

Distractions and generalizing

Training dogs to behave calmly in places pets are not permitted is the most challenging part of training a service dog. Service dogs are expected to ignore distractions and pay attention to their handlers in complex environments. Service dogs may work in office buildings, schools, public transportation and medical facilities, and may have to travel by air. Service dogs need to ignore distractions in a supermarket and lie quietly under a table in a restaurant. While service dogs work on leash in public places, they may need to very briefly work off leash in order to perform a task. Service dogs should always be attentive and responsive to their owners, regardless of what is happening around them.

Service dog candidates are prepared for public access work from young puppyhood through appropriate socialization experiences. Formal public access work begins more intensively when the dog is an older adolescent, usually between the ages of 1 and 2.

Owner-trainers tend to want to take their dogs out and about early. Service dog coaches are in the important role of educating owner-trainers about dog development. They need to help make sure owner-trainers do not rush the process or put undue pressure on young dogs.

Generalizing behaviors involves practice in increasingly different and complex environments and situations. As the service dog in training gains confidence, the dog will be asked to perform service dog tasks in these varied settings. The duration of the public access work increases as well.

Service dog coaches need to educate owners on how to handle their dogs in public access situations appropriately and discreetly. Because public access work can be stressful for dogs, owners need to learn how to identify when their dogs are stressed, in order to understand when and how to give their dogs a break. Owners must be able to ensure their dog's safety in complex settings. The owner always needs to be able to get the service dog's attention, even if the dog is distracted.

Owners also need to learn how to handle mishaps that can occur even with a well-trained service dog. Service dog coaches should educate owners on basic cleanup supplies owners should always have on hand. Owners also need education about fitting and maintaining their dogs' equipment. Last but not least, service dog coaches should prepare owners to appropriately answer questions from business owners.

Training the "at-home-only" service dog

Some people with disabilities benefit from a service dog who is trained only to help at home and does not work in places pets are not permitted. Some people with disabilities may only need a dog's help with activities of daily living in their home. Perhaps the owner works from home, is retired or does not work due to their disability. In other cases, the owner may have personal care attendants who come and go throughout the day. An at-home-only service dog's support can be invaluable during those time periods when there is not a personal care attendant available.

In many ways, an at-home-only service dog can be an ideal candidate for owner-training. It is an opportunity to train a dog to do helpful tasks without the pressure of public access. Some dogs who are not appropriate for public access work are wonderful candidates for at-home-only service dog work. In other cases, the owner may simply not have the time to train a dog to the level needed for public access and may benefit from a service dog's assistance with a few tasks at home.

Before agreeing to help train an at-home-only service dog, the trainer should be certain that the client understands why the dog is not being trained for public access. The owner should be in full agreement not to take the dog to places pets are not permitted. Otherwise, the trainer is risking that the owner will take the unprepared dog to a location that does not allow pets as a service dog. Written training notes, contracts and other forms of documentation can help protect trainers from liability and ensure that the owner and trainer are on the same page. Care and consideration in terms of task selection is still essential.

Service dog training is always customized

One of the exciting aspects of offering service dog coaching is that every owner-trainer and service dog candidate will be different. The approach is customized to each team.

Working with a new puppy

A person with a disability purchases a Labrador puppy from a breeder with a history of producing successful service dogs. The breeder helped the owner in choosing a puppy she felt would be a good match for service work.

This owner will need to start with the basics, including puppy training and socialization. The service dog coach can use this opportunity to get to know the owner and puppy in the context of puppy training classes. The classes allow for informal assessment of the pup's suitability for service work, as the trainer can observe the puppy over a period of time. The trainer also can start to educate the owner about what is involved in service dog training. After the puppy matures, the service dog coach can recommend private lessons, and possibly day training or board and train, to allow for a more thorough observation of the dog's suitability for service dog training.

Working with an adopted shelter dog

A person with a disability adopts a 9-month-old mixed-breed dog from a shelter and immediately contacts a service dog coach for help training the dog for service work. This owner needs education on the importance of allowing for settling-in time. The owner would benefit from learning strategies to reduce the dog's stress and help the dog adjust to the new environment. If the dog has no serious behavior problems, the dog may benefit from some basic training. This owner also needs education on what the behavior expectations are for service dogs and information on the service dog training process. After the owner has had the dog for a few months, the trainer and owner will have a better sense of what the dog's needs are and whether it is appropriate to move forward with an initial evaluation of the dog's suitability to work as a service dog.

Working with the family

A family with an 18-month-old dog who has already passed the American Kennel Club's Canine Good Citizen evaluation reaches out for help training the dog to support a child with a disability. The service dog coach can schedule a private lesson to conduct an initial evaluation of the dog's behavior and temperament and learn more about the child's needs. This might be a good candidate for moving forward with task training and public access, assuming the dog has the right temperament.

A service dog coach may see everything from retired show dogs to rescue dogs, from puppies to adults, and from totally green to already well underway in the training process. With the growth and expansion of service dog programs, pet dog trainers may even be sought for a second opinion or training support with a program-trained service dog.

The process of supporting an owner-trainer varies tremendously based on the needs of the dog, the owner and the training services that are available. The owner's ability to pay for training is also a factor. Private training appointments are always a part of the process, but in some cases board and train, day training and group classes may also be involved. Remote appointments via phone and web conferencing can be incorporated as well, and may be especially useful for providing basic information about the service dog training process. If the trainer only offers one or two types of training services, that may still be sufficient. Another option is to network with like-minded colleagues and collaborate on cases.

A sample training plan

A training plan is helpful for both the client and the trainer to set short-term and long-term goals. Of course, the training plan must be customized to the individual situation and flexible enough to allow for unexpected changes.

Here is an example of a training plan for a complete start-to-finish process beginning with a young puppy for mobility support. While time frames are not delineated, a typical time frame would be a little over two years:

1. Socialize the puppy to new places, dogs, people and situations, and complete a group puppy kindergarten class.

2. Complete group classes to firm up basic training. Work on loose-leash walking, Sits, Downs, Stays, attention to name, Recall and Leave It. Play Retrieve games.

3. Take a private lesson for an initial assessment of the dog's suitability for service dog training when the dog is approximately 8 months old.

4. Work toward the AKC Canine Good Citizen certificate. Take private lessons in pet-friendly locations to begin preparing the dog for public access training.

5. Begin to train a controlled service dog Retrieve in private lessons.

6. Begin formal task training. Enroll the dog in a day training package. The professional service dog coach can finish training the Retrieve, introduce additional tasks like Pull to open a door and Stand (a foundation behavior for brace work).

7. Begin public access training in private training lessons. Enroll the dog in a group rally class to help the owner continue to practice basic skills.

8. Conduct veterinary screenings to check for the dog's joint health. Measure the dog for a balance harness. Check in with the handler's physical therapist to select the harness handle height.

9. Train balance tasks with the harness in private lessons.

10. Work on generalizing public access training and task training to different situations and environments in private lessons.

11. Conduct assessments of public access training and task training in private lessons.

12. Transition the team to maintenance training through a combination of intermittent group classes and private lessons.

In the real world, it is rare for training plans to go this smoothly. Most of the time, there will be multiple glitches along the way. Some of the glitches may be training or behavior challenges that take longer to address than anticipated. For example, perhaps the dog starts to pull on leash persistently and the owner has difficulty with control. There may be a need for additional board and train or day training sessions to address the challenge, or more group or private lessons may be needed. It is also not uncommon for the owner to have health setbacks that impact how much the owner can work on the dog's training. Sometimes the health changes mean that the tasks selected need to be revisited. The dog's health is part of the picture as well. If this particular service dog candidate did not pass the veterinary screening, the dog would not be fitted with a harness and the bracing and balancing tasks would not be trained.

6

Service Dog
Task Selection

Tasks, those specific behaviors to help a person with a disability, are the key to what makes a service dog a service dog. Tasks needed vary as much as people with disabilities do. Task selection is not one size fits all, even for people with the same diagnosis. A task that may be very helpful for one person may be completely inappropriate for another.

As we learn more about the abilities of dogs and benefits of human-animal interaction, the task possibilities continue to grow. The tasks service dogs do are often grouped based on the kind of disability the dog is being trained to help with, such as mobility dog tasks, hearing dog tasks, guide dog tasks and so forth. In reality, each type of service dog is, in many ways, its own specialty. Service dog programs often focus on training a few types of service dogs.

Because the role of service dogs is expanding so quickly, some tasks performed by service dogs are very new. There is a real need for more scientific, objective research on these new tasks and roles for service dogs. Pet dog trainers new to service dog training should stick with low-risk tasks that are of clear benefit to the individual.

Task lists are often structured under discrete categories; however, in reality, disabilities do not occur in discrete categories. For instance, an individual may have both a mental illness and a physical disability. One of the unique advantages to service dogs as an accommodation for disability is their flexibility. A service dog may be able to be trained both for mobility support and hearing alert work, for example.

Service dog tasks categories

Before you can begin a detailed training plan for your owner-trainer client, you must come to a mutual understanding of which tasks the dog needs to learn. For practical purposes, tasks discussed in this section are organized based on categories of service dog work. However, in the real world, tasks are selected based on the individual's needs, not the category.

Mobility tasks

Mobility service dogs can be trained to help people with a wide range of disabilities. Everything from neurological conditions and autoimmune diseases to injuries may affect a person's ability to move. Some people with mobility impairments may use adaptive equipment like wheelchairs and walkers. Others may not require any adaptive equipment. Even people with the same diagnosis may be affected very differently and require different tasks.

The Retrieve is the fundamental mobility service dog task. This is also an essential task for most service dogs of all types. As you'll learn in Chapter 7, the service dog Retrieve is very different from a Retrieve taught to a pet dog in play or as a trick. In most cases the dog needs to deliver the item directly to the person's hand, but the dog may deliver the item to the person's lap if the person has limited use of their hands. The behavior must be trained very precisely and be very controlled.

The components of the Retrieve behavior include taking the item, holding the item, carrying the item and delivering the item to the person's hand. These components can individually be put on cues: Take, Hold, Carry and Give. Then the components can be combined to train additional mobility service dog tasks. For example, Take and Hold are combined with Pull to train a dog to pull a zipper, remove clothing or open a door. Take, Hold and Carry can be used when the dog carries a bag for the owner.

Mobility service dogs also may need to push buttons for elevators, lights and accessible door open buttons. They also may need to push to close doors and cabinets. Push may be performed with a nose or paw.

Mobility service dogs are also often taught to respond should their handler fall. The needed response may vary depending on the situation. The dog may be taught to retrieve a phone, press an emergency call button, lie down by the handler or retrieve an assistive device. Some dogs are also trained to help the person get up from a fall.

Providing direct support to a person walking or pulling a wheelchair are commonly requested mobility service dog tasks. These and other tasks requiring the dog to directly support the individual may be risky for both the handler and for the dog. Dogs being asked to perform physically demanding tasks will often need to be retired from service work more quickly. A healthcare provider who is qualified to assess the safety of the task for the person, such as a physical therapist, should be consulted to ensure the task is appropriate for the individual. Veterinarians and veterinary orthopedists' input should be consulted before training physically demanding tasks like balance, brace and wheelchair pulling.

Adaptive equipment can often provide direct support in a safer, more reliable way than a service dog. Technology continues to expand options for people with disabilities. Power-assist devices can be attached to wheelchairs to provide help in moving up hills or for long distances if a full-power wheelchair is not practical.

Hearing dog tasks

In contrast to mobility dogs, hearing dogs respond to a change in the environment rather than cues from the owner. Hearing dogs need to respond to different sounds by alerting their owners.

A hearing dog often performs alerts by touching the owner with a nose or paw, and also may lead the owner to the sound source. A dog who has the right temperament and behavior for hearing alert work will quickly generalize the training and alert the owner to a variety of sounds. Great hearing dogs even alert to novel sounds that were not previously trained. This behavior can be potentially life-saving. Importantly, hearing dogs alert to sounds like fire alarms and sirens.

Hearing dogs may be needed to be persistent in alerting, for instance, if it is necessary to wake the owner in the case of a fire alarm. They also need to be taught to alert the owner when another person says the owner's name.

In addition to sound-alerting, hearing dogs are also often trained to retrieve some items. Hearing dogs may be trained to retrieve without a cue, for example to pick up the leash or the owner's keys if these items are accidentally dropped.

Tasks for disabilities that impact emotions, behavior or cognition

A wide range of disabilities can impact emotions, behavior or cognition. Mental illness, neurological disorders, developmental disorders and traumatic brain injuries fall into this broad category. The tasks that may be helpful range as widely as the disabilities in this group do. Tasks are often selected with the goals of helping the individual refocus, calm down or remember. Other tasks that may be needed include alerting a caregiver that help is needed or interrupting compulsive behaviors.

There are tasks from other service dog specialty areas that may be needed as well. For instance, people with a mental illness, neurological condition or developmental disorder may face physical challenges like balance problems or fatigue due to the disability or as a side effect from medication needed. They may then need mobility tasks, Retrieves or balance support.

Additionally, behaviors like turning on lights may be very helpful if a person is anxious in a dark room, or alternatively, needs lights turned off to calm down. Some guide tasks such as finding an exit, finding the owner's car in a parking lot, or leading the owner home may be needed for people with conditions that affect memory or thinking. Even hearing alert behaviors such as alerting to alarms and alerting to the person's name may be helpful. Some people may need the dog to help them wake up or focus in a distracting or stressful setting.

Reminder behaviors can be helpful as well. A dog may be trained to touch the individual with a paw or nose to remind the person to take medication. If the dog is working with a two-person team, the dog may perform a task cued by a caregiver to assist the individual with a disability. A caregiver may cue the service dog to deliver a bottle of juice to encourage an individual with dementia to drink, for example.

Service dogs may be trained to lie down on or lean on a person on cue to provide comfort or help a person relax. Smaller service dogs may be trained to simply jump on the person's lap on cue.

Tricks may even be helpful for service dogs for seniors with dementia or children. The tricks cued by the individual or by a caregiver may help distract or calm.

Alert and response tasks

The area of medical alert work has generated excitement in the service dog world. These tasks range from diabetic alert to seizure alert, allergen alert and more. At the moment we have more questions than answers about medical alert tasks. Are the alerts able to be substantiated by objective research? Which dogs can be trained to alert? Are dogs reliable at performing alerts in real-world contexts? What are dogs responding to when they alert? What are the best methods to train dogs to alert?

Alerting to seizures has been considered by many in the service dog industry as a natural behavior that some service dogs may offer spontaneously, rather than as a trained behavior per se. However, there are some trainers who believe there may be an odor dogs can be trained to respond to. As with many alert behaviors, there is a need for objective scientific research on seizure alerting. It's important to be aware that causes and types of seizures vary greatly. Given the numerous questions about alert behavior for seizures, service dog trainers have often opted to train dogs to *respond* to seizures rather than to alert to them. Trained responses to seizures or other medical events may include bringing a phone, bringing medication, pressing a call button to alert that help is needed or lying down next to the owner to provide comfort.

Diabetic alert dogs are trained to let the owner know when they have noticed a change in the owner's blood sugar levels by touching the owner. Trainers may teach the dogs to respond to a change in the odor of the owner's saliva. The dog may also be trained to retrieve medication or bring the owner juice. Additionally, the service dog may be trained to perform other tasks such as alerting a caregiver that help is needed. As with other types of medical alert work, there are questions about how reliable dogs really are at performing alerts to changes in owners' blood sugar. An excellent resource for trainers interested in this type of service dog work is *Training Your Diabetic Alert Dog* by Rita Martinez and Sue Barns.

Dogs' natural sensitivity to body language is an advantage when training them to perform anxiety alerts. Anxiety alerts can be trained by teaching the dog to respond to subtle visual cues in the person's behavior by touching the person with a nose or paw. For example, if the person taps their foot when they start to become anxious, then the foot tapping becomes the cue for the dog to perform the alert. The dog's alert can help the owner become aware of the need to take measures to reduce their anxiety. Similarly, small changes in the owner's behavior before other mental health events, such as panic attacks, can become cues for the dog to perform either an alert or response behavior.

People describe service dogs as being able to alert to various medical events and odors: migraines, blood pressure changes, food allergens, allergens in the environment and autoimmune conditions. There is growing research in using dogs' olfactory skills for alerts. It is important to remember that research showing that dogs can alert to various odors in a laboratory setting does not automatically transfer to real-world service dog work where the dog is working long hours around many distractions. The medical community is looking with increased scrutiny at the claims made about service dogs, so more objective research should be forthcoming. Depending on the situation, there may be medical consequences, possibly even life-threatening ones, if a dog fails to alert. This is not an area for an inexperienced service dog trainer.

Guide dog tasks

Guide dog training is another area that requires experience and high-level service dog training skills because it is exceptionally high-risk. If the dog makes an error, the dog could lead a person into a road, cause them to trip and fall, or worse. Examples of some guide tasks include turning right and left on verbal cues, walking in a straight line ahead of the owner, leading a person to a door, automatically stopping at curbs and alerting a person to an object in their path.

Guide dog work is a unique specialty and is also not an area for an inexperienced service dog trainer. Because of the uniqueness of the tasks and needs involved in training guide dogs, organizations that train these dogs often do so exclusively. This is unlike other service dog programs, which often train several different types of service dogs. Additionally, given the difficulty accommodating training for people who are blind, people who need a guide dog are usually best served by applying to a high-quality service dog program that specializes in guide dogs.

There are situations where a person may benefit from a few guide dog tasks without needing a full guide dog, such as an owner who has a vision impairment or limitation but is not blind. Understanding the subtle ways vision limitations affect the owner is still important. Working in collaboration with a rehabilitation specialist trained in supporting people with vision limitations, such as an occupational therapist, can be invaluable in ensuring that the training is appropriate and safe.

Considerations in selecting service dog tasks

"I found a list of a dozen different tasks online that I need my service dog to do. We can train these in four weeks, right? I know my dog is super smart."

Usually owner-trainers approach the dog trainer with a very long list of tasks in mind. Owner-trainers often choose tasks based on information they learned online, on the news or on social media. Pet dog trainers should not assume that the tasks that an owner-trainer wishes to train their service dog to perform are necessarily appropriate. The owner-trainer's list is often a great starting point for the conversation on choosing tasks. Sometimes owners may not be aware of some additional behaviors that a dog could do to help. However, most of the time the task lists the owner approaches the trainer with will need to be reduced in length, and tasks will need to be prioritized.

Trainers should not assume that owners have discussed these tasks with their healthcare provider. In fact, in my experience, it is very rare for this conversation to take place. Adding to the challenge is the reality that healthcare providers themselves may not be aware of ways a service dog can help or may not realize the limitations of a service dog. It is to the owner and service dog's benefit for everyone to be on the same page. The service dog coach, owner and healthcare provider should all work together to determine which tasks are needed and appropriate.

Always consider, what are the consequences if the dog makes a mistake? Alternative tasks may be safer. For example, if it is too risky for the owner to use the dog to brace when getting up from a chair, the dog may be able to be trained to bring a walker closer to the owner or alert a caregiver if the owner falls. Service dogs are not always the answer. The owner may need to work with his or her healthcare provider to find the most appropriate ways to address the challenge.

It is easy to see how tasks like wheelchair pulling or bracing may pose risks for people with mobility impairments. It may be less obvious to see how some tasks may be inappropriate for people with mental illness or other disabilities that affect emotions and cognition. Consider training a dog to interrupt a compulsive behavior. What if the owner-trainer has to rehearse the compulsive behavior as part of the dog's training practice? What is the effect of the task training process on the person's mental health? Owner-trainers with post-traumatic stress disorder may request a task that makes them feel safer, like cuing the dog to stand between themselves and others. However, whether tasks like this are genuinely helpful to a person's mental health is debated in the industry. Communication with the client's licensed mental health professional is important to make sure the chosen tasks and training are right for the individual.

There are also service dog tasks that may be risky or stressful for the dog, person or both. Tethering a dog to a child or training a dog to physically prevent a child or adult from engaging in an unsafe behavior are examples. The dog's needs always matter. In addition to posing risks to the individual, tethering can be stressful for the dog and put the dog in a situation where an individual may react inappropriately toward the dog.

Just because a service dog program somewhere trains dogs to perform a particular task, does not mean the task is appropriate or safe. It is important to keep in mind that service dog programs vary in quality, and there is little and sometimes no objective research about many of the newer types of service dogs.

Service, not protection!

No service dog should be trained for protection work. Aggressive behavior is never appropriate in a service dog.

7

Task Training Foundations

While there are an endless variety of possible service dog tasks, there are some common foundation behaviors that are needed for many of them. These foundation behaviors can be recombined for a variety of different tasks.

Clicker training is the best way to teach a dog a behavior very precisely. If you are unfamiliar with clicker training, jump to the Resources section for some excellent introductory books on this topic.

Some basic training tools are needed for task training, including a clicker, soft, small-sized training treats, a container to hold the treats and a willing dog, of course. Additional training tools are needed for some service dog tasks. Service dog trainers often use gadgets in training that are not typically used in dog training. For instance, used cell phones, old remote controls, touch lights, push buttons and even door knobs may be valuable for training some tasks and behaviors.

As with other training, new behaviors are best started in a quiet location with no distractions. Verbal cues for behaviors are introduced when the dog is offering the desired behavior predictably. Say the cue right before the dog offers the behavior. Training sessions should be brief and enjoyable for both the dog and the trainer.

Giving service dogs choices

Asking a service dog to perform behaviors that are unpleasant or anxiety-provoking for the dog runs the risk of damaging the service dog's relationship with the owner over the long term. There are nearly always multiple ways to achieve the same goal, and it is important to look for options that work for both the owner and the dog.

For example, some service dogs are trained to lie down on an individual to help the person relax or to reduce physical pain. This task, referred to as deep pressure therapy, is commonly requested for children with autism and for people who have mental illness. While some dogs are born lap dogs and enjoy this type of contact, not all dogs are comfortable lying down on a person. If the person the dog is being asked to lie down on is already upset, it might even be unsafe. Alternatives should be considered. The dog could lean on the person or retrieve a weighted blanket, for instance.

Another way to give a service dog in training a choice is to allow the dog to have some control over the way the task is performed. For instance, teach the dog two ways to push an elevator button, with a paw and with the nose. Then, allow the dog to choose either approach when performing the behavior in the environment. It makes no impact on the end result for the person, and the dog may much prefer doing it one way versus another.

Targeting

What do a hearing dog alerting to a sound, a guide dog stopping at a curb, a diabetic alert dog alerting to a blood sugar change and a mobility service dog closing a cabinet door have in common? Targeting is a component of each of these tasks. Targeting involves training the dog to touch something with a part of their body. In the case of a hearing alert or diabetic alert dog, the dog usually touches the handler with a nose or paw. Similarly, the dog may close a cabinet by pushing the cabinet door with a nose or paw. Guide dogs can be trained to touch the curb with their front feet. Targeting is an essential foundation skill for service dogs and has many applications. The simplest form of Target training involves teaching the dog to touch your hand with their nose. Here are the steps in training a dog to perform this behavior.

1. Hold a smelly treat in a closed fist. Hold your hand a few inches away from the dog's nose. Keep your hand still, do not move your hand toward or away from the dog. Click and treat when the dog's nose touches your fist. Deliver the treat by opening your hand. Move your hand away from the dog after each repetition.

2. Repeat Step 1 a few times until the dog is quickly touching your hand.

3. Increase the distance between your hand and the dog's nose by a few inches. Click and open your hand to give the treat when the dog's nose touches your hand.

4. Repeat Step 3. When the dog is performing Step 3 easily, add the verbal cue "Touch."

5. Repeat the process but without a treat in your hand. Instead, using the same hand the dog touched, pick up a treat from a container and deliver the treat after you click.

When beginning to teach Targeting, hold your hand
so the dog can easily reach.

This behavior can be expanded after the dog is performing reliably. Owners can transfer the behavior to having the dog touch their leg by holding their hand on their leg for several repetitions. Then they can move their hand away in small increments and differentially mark and reward only when the dog touches their leg and not their hand.

Dogs can be taught to target with their paws instead of their noses by placing a target, such as a touch light, on the floor. First, mark and reward as the dog approaches it. Differentially mark and reward behaviors that are closer to the objective. Only click and reward when the dog steps close to the target and lastly, only when the dog steps directly on the target.

To train a dog to close a cabinet on the cue "Push," the dog needs to be able to perform the Touch reliably on a cue. You also need a plastic lid and a cabinet door that is very easy for the dog to close. Here are the steps to teach a dog to close a cabinet.

1. Use the cue "Touch" to get the dog to target your hand. Click and treat.

2. Hold a lid in the same hand your dog touched. If needed, you can make the lid more appealing by smearing a little peanut butter on it. Click and treat when the dog touches the lid. Move to the next step when the dog is touching the lid reliably.

3. Affix the lid to a cabinet that is easy to close. Begin with the cabinet door closed. Click and treat when the dog touches the lid. You may need to put your hand near the lid a few times to help the dog.

4. Open the cabinet very slightly, barely an inch, so it closes right away when the dog touches it. Click and treat when the dog closes the cabinet. Add the cue "Push." Cue the dog to sit and stay, and then reward the Stay with a treat before each repetition so the dog waits, allowing you to open the cabinet again.

5. Repeat Step 4 and slowly increase how wide you open the cabinet door with each repetition.

This training process can be adapted for accessible door open buttons, elevator buttons and some types of light switches.

*Choosing the right cabinet is important. This one
is both easy for the dog to reach and easy to close.*

The Retrieve

Retrieving is an essential task for many service dogs. The components of the Retrieve are required for everything from picking up dropped objects to bringing an emergency phone, opening doors and assisting with dressing.

The Retrieve needed of a service dog is distinctly different than the behavior needed for a pet dog in play and even of a trained trick dog. Dogs chew and shake items when they play with them. This could damage the item. Service dogs should not drop a cell phone or bite down hard on a bottle of medication while retrieving. When performing a trick, the dog may only be trained to retrieve particular materials. Service dogs need to be able to pick up various items of different textures and materials. They need to hold the item carefully. Service dogs need to turn their heads to carefully pick up bottles from a counter, or the bottle can fall and roll. Service dogs may need to use their front teeth when picking up a pencil, but their back teeth to firmly hold a tether. If the dog's behavior is not carefully controlled, it can be unsafe.

The finished retrieve should look like this:

1. Cue "Take," and the dog picks up the item you point to.

2. Cue "Bring," and the dog carries the item to you.

3. Cue "Hold," and the dog holds the item without moving.

4. Cue "Give," and the dog releases the item into your hand.

Remember that service dogs are usually trained to deliver items directly to the owner's hand. If the owner has impaired control of their hands, the dog may be trained to hold the item for a longer period of time before releasing so the owner can secure it, or the dog may be taught to drop the item on the owner's lap.

Additional training tools needed for Retrieve work include wooden dumbbells or dowels. The dumbbell or dowel should be an item that is comfortable and easy for the dog to grab and hold. Be aware that material, weight and texture can make a big difference when training this task. Get several different kinds of dumbbells and dowels so you are ready. Obedience dumbbells can be purchased online and wooden dowels can easily be purchased in hardware stores.

Training the dog to hold the item in their mouth without chewing or dropping it is the hardest part of this behavior. It is important to keep all training practice sessions short and fun. Training this behavior is an advanced skill for a professional trainer. The training recipe for the service dog Retrieve needs to be adjusted according to the individual dog's responses.

1. Hold the dumbbell in front of the dog. Click and treat when the dog shows any interest in it. Move the dumbbell away and repeat until the dog is readily touching the dumbbell with his nose. If the dog is hesitant, you can try smearing a little peanut butter or cheese on the rod of the dumbbell.

2. Click and treat when the dog puts their teeth on the dumbbell. Repeat until the dog does this quickly.

3. Click and treat when the dog grabs the dumbbell. Make sure you are clicking the moment the dog's teeth are on the dumbbell. Repeat until the dog is immediately grabbing the dumbbell.

4. Add the cue "Take." Continue to repeat Step 3, but slowly delay before clicking and treating. Build duration on the Hold.

5. When the dog is holding the dumbbell for at least three seconds, start letting go of the dumbbell. Begin by only momentarily letting go of the dumbbell. Make sure you have one hand on the dumbbell again when you click. Give the dog a treat. Repeat the process, slowly increasing the amount of time you are not holding the dumbbell.

6. When the dog is holding the dumbbell for at least five seconds easily, add the cue for Hold by saying "Hold" right after you say "Take."

7. Start teaching the dog to move toward your hand with the dumbbell. Cue "Take, Hold," let go of the dumbbell and move your hand just a few inches away from the dog. When the dog moves the dumbbell to your hand, click and treat. If the dog does not move toward you, try taking a step or two backward right after saying "Take." Pat your legs or clap to encourage the dog to move toward you.

8. Repeat Step 7 while slowly increasing the distance between the dog's nose and your hand. Work toward having the dog move a foot or two toward you while holding the dumbbell.

9. When the dog is readily taking the dumbbell, holding it, moving toward you with the dumbbell in his mouth at least one foot, and giving it to your hand, add the cue for Give. Say "Give" the instant before the dog places the dumbbell in your hand.

10. Begin working toward having the dog pick up the dumbbell from the ground. Start by offering the dumbbell with your hand held a few inches below the dog's nose. Cue "Take" and "Give," and click and treat.

11. Repeat Step 10 while offering the dumbbell increasingly closer to the ground before saying "Take." Repeat until the dog is directly picking up the dumbbell from the ground.

12. Combine taking the dumbbell from the ground with having the dog carry it. Start to place the dumbbell farther away to increase the distance between the dog and dumbbell. Point to

the dumbbell when you cue "Take." Work slowly to ensure the behavior is precise. You may have to cue "Sit, Stay," and reward the dog for staying while you place the dumbbell on the ground. Add the cue by saying "Bring" as the dog is moving toward you with the dumbbell.

A common training mistake is to let go of the dumbbell too soon. It is better to wait until the dog is clearly beginning to hold.

Often trainers find getting a reliable Take and Hold difficult. For dogs who are hesitant to take, it may help to get a little excited and trigger some play behavior during the training sessions. Moving the dumbbell toward the dog can be intimidating for some dogs. Instead, hold the dumbbell steady and allow the dog to move toward it. Experimenting with dumbbells or dowels of different materials and widths may also be helpful. Timing with the clicker is essential. The trainer must time the click at the exact instant that the dumbbell is in the dog's teeth.

For dogs who mouth the dumbbell when learning the Hold behavior, it can help to delay clicking until the dog is no longer mouthing. Sometimes changing the width or texture of the item you are working with helps the dog learn to hold without mouthing. Most dogs will be more likely to mouth a smaller, narrower item and less likely to mouth a wider one. Another strategy is to pull gently on the dumbbell when it is in the dog's mouth to encourage a firmer or longer Hold. Yet another strategy that sometimes works is to have the dog sitting or lying down before cueing "Take" and "Hold."

Timing is essential, and trainers new to teaching this behavior often click late. The click must occur at the exact moment the dog is holding the dumbbell. Clicking after the dog releases the dumbbell will teach the dog that releasing, not holding, is the desired behavior.

Some additional common training errors include using a floppy item for training a new dog. This encourages the dog to play with rather than hold the item. Also, rushing through the process is a common mistake that will result in a sloppy behavior. It is better to proceed slowly than to end up having to retrain this skill or having the dog practice unwanted behaviors, like mouthing, that later have to be eliminated. Trainers who have not taught this behavior before will often need a full month or longer to do so. Fortunately, it only takes that long the first time. As trainers gain practice this quickly becomes easier to train.

Generalizing the Retrieve also takes time. Trainers need to work with service dog candidates with many different items on different surfaces and in different contexts. For some items, like bottles or containers on counters, the dog's head needs to turn in order for the dog to pick it up without knocking the item over. Trainers can teach dogs to turn their heads to pick up a vertical object by placing a dumbbell on its side on a table. A flat-sided dumbbell that can stand on its own when placed this way is needed. The trainer can place one hand on top end of the dumbbell to secure it while cuing "Take." Click early for a few repetitions, when the dog's head turns. Then fade the use of the hand on the dumbbell.

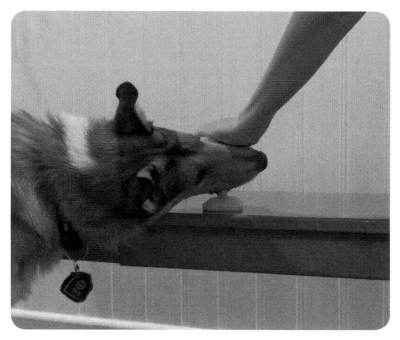

Placing the dumbbell on a low bench makes it easier for the dog to learn how to turn his head and grab it.

Remember to work on each of the component behaviors of the Retrieve: Take, Hold, Carry and Give. Take time to train each component behavior carefully so the dog performs precisely. Each component can be combined with some additional behaviors to teach additional tasks.

Training the Pull behavior

Adding the Pull behavior to Take and Hold teaches the dog to perform helpful behaviors like opening doors with a tether. You will need a dumbbell, a tether made of a soft material that the dog is comfortable holding, and a door to work with. Fleece or flannel are good materials for the tether. The door needs to be easily opened by pulling; cabinet and refrigerator doors are good candidates. The dog needs to already know how to perform all of the Retrieve components before you begin teaching this behavior.

1. Cue the dog to "Take" and "Hold" the dumbbell. Do not release the dumbbell with your hands; instead pull gently against the dog. When the dog pulls back, click and treat right away. You want to click quickly, so you mark slight controlled tension, not out-of-control pulling.

2. Repeat Step 1 until the dog is pulling steadily in a controlled way. Add the verbal cue by saying "Pull" after saying "Hold."

3. Hold the tether in front of the dog the same way you held the dumbbell. Cue "Take," "Hold" and "Pull," and click and treat when the dog pulls the tether. Repeat until the dog is performing easily.

4. Secure one end of the tether to the doorknob. Hold the other end of the tether. Say "Take," "Hold" and "Pull." Click and treat when the dog pulls open the door. Repeat until the dog is performing this easily.

5. Repeat Step 4, but do not hold the tether yourself. Say "Take," "Hold" and "Pull." Click and treat when the dog pulls the door open.

6. Slowly work to increase your distance from the door so the dog can go away from you to the tether, then perform Take, Hold and Pull to open the door.

*There are important details to consider when training a
dog to open doors, for example, the angle at which
the dog needs to pull and how much force is needed.*

Train the dog to put an item in a trash bin

Service dogs often need to put items in other locations. The same
Retrieve components can be combined to train the dog to put items
in the trash. You will need the dumbbell, some trash and a trash bin.
The Retrieve behavior needs to be reliable with a variety of items
before you train this behavior. Start with an easy trash bin, one that is
open at the top. If you have previously trained dogs to put toys away
in a basket, this process will be familiar to you.

1. Cue the dog to retrieve the dumbbell from the floor as a
   warm-up.

2. With a trash bin in front of you, cue the dog to retrieve the
   dumbbell, but this time put your hand inside the bin before
   cuing "Give." Click and reward when the dog puts the dumbbell in your hand.

3. Repeat Step 2 until the dog is performing this behavior easily. Keep your hand open when the dog puts the dumbbell in your hand, so it falls into the bin.

4. Repeat Step 3 and start to work toward having your hand outside of the bin by incrementally moving your hand out of the bin with each repetition. Click when the dumbbell is still being placed in the bin. Introduce the cue "Trash" instead of "Give."

5. Cue "Take" and "Trash" and click and treat when the dumbbell is placed in the bin. Slowly increase your distance from the bin with each repetition until you are able to cue the dog to put the dumbbell in the bin from anywhere within the room.

6. Repeat the process but with actual trash.

When looking for a trash bin to begin training this behavior, the height is important. This bin allows the dog to easily reach in to drop the item.

Alerting to a sound

Alert work involves the dog either responding to a change in the environment or to a change in the handler's body. Dogs can be trained to alert to things they see, hear or smell. Dogs usually are trained to alert by touching the owner with a paw or nose. Alert dogs need to be trained to be persistent if the owner is distracted.

To train a dog to alert the handler to the sound of a phone ringing, you will need two phones (one to trigger the other phone to ring), a clicker and treats. The dog also needs to have been previously trained to touch the owner's leg on the verbal cue "Touch." It is important that no visual signal is needed for the dog to touch the owner's leg. It must be solidly on the verbal cue alone.

1. Ring the phone—make sure the dog cannot see you do this. You can hold your hand with the phone out of the dog's line of sight. Say "Touch" and click and treat when the dog touches your leg. Repeat this process until the dog starts to anticipate and touches your leg when the phone rings, before you say "Touch."

2. Ring the phone. Do not say "Touch." Wait for the dog to touch your leg, then click and treat. If the dog does not touch your leg, then verbally cue "Touch" and repeat the first step again.

3. Practice with distractions. Ring the phone at random times of the day in different parts of the home.

As you can see, this is actually a straightforward behavior to train. However, if a dog does not have the temperament needed for hearing work, the dog will not be likely to offer this behavior in real-world situations. This is true even if the dog responds in a training context. For hearing work, it is essential to have a dog who naturally tends to notice sounds in the environment.

Training the dog to lead the owner to the sound source requires some extra steps. The phone that is ringing should be at least 3 feet away. The treats should be located next to the phone that is ringing. The dog needs to have been previously trained to alert to the sound of the phone ringing.

1. Ring the phone. When the dog touches you, click and then go to the phone that was ringing to reward the dog with the treats.

2. Repeat Step 1 until the dog is starting to move toward the ringing phone quickly after the click, ahead of you.

3. Move the phone that rings farther away and repeat the process. Start to follow the dog to the ringing phone rather than moving ahead of the dog. As the dog improves, continue to repeat, increasing the distance with each repetition.

4. Add distractions and vary the times of day when you practice.

Response tasks

In the case of a response behavior, the cue is something the owner does rather than a verbal cue or hand signal. For example, if the owner needs the dog to perform a specific task when they fall, the owner's fall is the cue. Response tasks are important for many types of service dogs. People with seizures, mental illness, mobility problems and even people with some sensory disabilities may need the dog to perform a response task.

Many dog trainers are used to training dogs to respond to hand signals. Consider the owner falling down to be a very big hand signal. A common response taught to some service dogs is for the dog to lie down next to the owner if the owner falls. This behavior can be helpful if the owner is in public, as the dog will automatically wait near the owner, ready for the owner to give another cue. If the person is anxious, stressed or confused by the fall, having the service dog by their side can be comforting. Lying down if the owner falls is also usually safer for the dog if the team is in public. It helps ensure that the dog remains by the owner rather than wandering off. As you practice, of course, be safe. There is no need for anyone to literally make themselves fall. Good acting skills are a plus.

The Down must be reliable on a verbal cue before training this behavior. To ensure the behavior is reliable on a verbal cue, practice with the dog when you are in different positions. Cue the Down when you are sitting, when your back is to the dog and when you are a few feet away from the dog. When the dog is performing reliably, you can begin teaching the dog to respond to your "fall."

To keep it fun and easy for the puppy, I cued "Down" when I was facing the puppy first, and then I repeated it after moving my chair.

1. Lie down on the floor, cue the dog to Down, and click and treat. Stand up and repeat until the dog starts to anticipate the cue and lies down as soon as you begin to lie down.

2. Lie down on the floor, wait for the dog to lie down, click and treat. If the dog does not lie down after ten seconds of waiting, say "Down," and click and treat. Then stand up and repeat Step 1 for longer before moving on.

3. Repeat the process, but begin changing your position slightly as you lie down. For instance, instead of lying down flat on your back, lie down on your side.

4. Repeat Step 3 but change your position again. Try lying down facing forward.

5. Repeat Step 3 with changing *how* you lie down. For instance, start walking and suddenly lie down, stand up from a chair and suddenly lie down. This is time for your acting skills. Call out "oops!" as you lie down. Practice carefully, so you do not get hurt.

6. Help the dog generalize the skill. Carefully practice "falling" many different ways. Practice with distractions and in different locations.

There are a wide range of different response tasks that can be trained. For instance, dogs may be trained to pick up a leash if the person accidentally drops it. The dog may be trained to alert the caregiver with a paw or nose touch if a child with a disability has a seizure.

Many owner-trainers want the dog to bring them an emergency phone. Sometimes owners want this trained as a response task and other times they want this on a verbal cue. In practice, it is important that the dog has easy access to the phone. Securely closed doors can make it impossible for the dog to perform this task. As with many aspects of service dog work, troubleshoot and have a Plan B in place in case the unexpected happens.

8

Public Access Training

Training service dog candidates to behave appropriately in public areas where pets are not normally permitted is the most challenging aspect of service dog training. Service dogs need to behave in ways that are not natural for dogs, for long periods of time in complex settings. Service dogs are expected to be able to perform reliably even if they are in a distracting location for the very first time. Whether in a supermarket, airport, school, office or bus, the service dog should be calm, responsive to their owner and ready to perform necessary tasks.

Assessing readiness for public access training

Owner-trainers usually want to put vests on their young in-training dogs and take them to no-pets-allowed locations as soon as possible. One of your most important tasks as a service dog coach is to determine when and how to transition a service dog candidate to work in public areas. These are challenging environments to work in as compared to the owner's home or a dog training facility. Ultimately the owner-trainer will need to be able to work with the dog in different places. You may need to conduct a combination of evaluations and observations to assess a team's readiness. Single evaluations are limited and only give a snapshot of a team's performance. Repeated observations and assessments over a period of time in a wide variety of settings provide a more accurate picture of the team's performance.

You will also need to be able to assess when the owner-trainer and service dog are ready to work independently, without your direct guidance and supervision. Public access training requires clients to frequently take their dog out to a variety of locations. Be aware that transportation poses challenges for some people with disabilities.

Finding locations to train before acquiring the vest

While a service-dog-in-training vest is usually required for places like supermarkets and restaurants, in many areas there are pet-friendly stores and shops where you can begin to prepare a service dog candidate for public access work. Hardware stores, garden centers, book stores, bus stations, shops and boutiques may be dog friendly and can serve as terrific environments to socialize a service dog candidate. Check with the store manager before assuming a location is pet friendly. Delaying having owner-trainers use a vest and holding off on no-pets-allowed locations until you are certain the dog is appropriate for public access, can go a long way to help prevent heartache. Remind clients they need to follow state and local laws when it comes to access for their service dog in training.

Expectations for the dog's behavior in public

While service dogs do not need to maintain the intense, focused attention seen in competition obedience, they do need to pay consistent attention to their owners, and be ready to perform needed tasks in spite of distractions. With the rising number of service dogs in public, now more than ever it is essential for service dogs to ignore other animals. Service dogs should never show aggression nor predatory behavior toward other animals of any species. Service dog candidates need to be trained to ignore other dogs, including dogs who may exhibit inappropriate behaviors like barking.

A saying often repeated in the service dog world is that the service dog should be "invisible." While invisible is a lot to ask for, service dogs should be discreet in public. They should not behave in ways that attract attention. Behaviors like barking, jumping on people, leash-pulling and soliciting interaction are inappropriate. Remember, aggression in any form is completely inappropriate for a service dog. Service dogs who soil or urinate in a no-pets-allowed building or in any building or inappropriate location should be removed immediately from the situation. Teach clients to implement a routine of giving the dog an opportunity to eliminate in an appropriate location before entering a building. It helps for owner-trainers to train the dog to eliminate on cue, as it is very inconvenient if the dog takes a long time to eliminate.

The working distance for service dogs varies depending on the adaptive equipment the owner uses, the situation and the owner's disability needs. In most cases the dog should be within a foot or two of the owner while working in public access. Service dogs should usually be walking on a loose leash. Two exceptions are dogs who pull wheelchairs and guide dogs. Both will obviously have some tension on their harnesses and may be farther away from their handlers. There may be circumstances when an owner needs to briefly drop the leash to allow the dog to perform a service dog task that requires a few feet of additional distance. However, these moments really are exceptions rather than rules. The vast majority of the time, service dogs should be on leash. Owner-trainers may also drop the dog's leash due to their disabilities or simply by accident. You can work with your client to train the dog to pick up the leash automatically if this occurs.

Dogs' behavior in restaurants and shops

In restaurants and coffee shops, service dogs need to lie down quietly under a table so that they are out of the way. They also need to ignore food that may be dropped or close by. It is not appropriate to feed a service dog in a restaurant under a table, so trainers need to set up opportunities to practice in settings where food rewards can be used. Tables of various heights with plates of food can be set up in a training facility or in the client's home to introduce and practice needed behaviors.

Service dogs should not shake off after standing back up near patrons eating at a restaurant. One way to prevent the dog from shaking off is to cue a behavior that is incompatible with shaking off until the team is no longer near other people. There are many possible behaviors that your client can cue. For instance, your client can cue a sustained

Nose Touch, a Chin Rest on the client's hand, a focused Heel or a Stand-Stay to prevent the dog from shaking off.

Service dogs also need to ignore merchandise and food items in stores, and should not solicit interaction with the public. Controlled practice opportunities for service dog candidates are important. In a dog training facility or other similar setting, you can set up a series of stations with distractions for clients to practice. The distractions might include stuffed animals, a low-height table with a plate of food, a toy shopping cart and a person making funny sounds. Be creative in changing distractions to help clients work on their skills. As always, be ready to make things easier by having your client work the dog farther away from the distractions if needed.

Attention with distractions

Because service dog owners are going about their lives when they work with their dogs in public places, they are not monitoring their dogs constantly. As a result, there are many situations when a working service dog will notice a distraction before the owner does. Marking and rewarding un-cued, offered attention helps a service dog candidate learn to give attention to the owner when the dog sees the distraction first. To begin, click and treat when the dog looks at the owner. Start working on this behavior in a setting with few distractions. Working in front of a mirror or reflective window allows the client to click and reward the dog for checking in when there is a distraction while the client is not looking at the dog. With practice, service dog candidates can learn to offer attention to their owners even when they encounter a significant distraction like another dog.

Unexpected demands

Every individual's lifestyle varies, and the service dog's public access demands may vary as well. Dogs being prepared for public access, however, need to be prepared for all settings and situations. Too often owners underestimate their needs and the ease of their lifestyle.

They may say, "I have a quiet lifestyle and don't go anywhere," and then suddenly share that they need their service dog to travel with them overseas.

Additionally, circumstances can change. Someone who is working at home and rarely travels may suddenly acquire a job that requires frequent travel. A person may be hospitalized and expect that their service dog will be with them. It is safer to assume that the client will have a complex lifestyle rather than inadequately prepare the service dog.

These high expectations can come at a cost for service dogs. Some service dog candidates who start out doing well in this role will start to show signs of stress later in their working careers. Service dog trainers have an important role in advocating for the dog. The service dog's owner needs to be prepared to meet the dog's needs and actively take steps to prevent stress-related behavior problems from surfacing down the road.

Owners may need to be reminded to praise their dog, even in public. I encourage and smile at my service dog when he checks in with me.

Expectations for the owner

Service dog owners need a strong skill set in order to handle their dog appropriately. An advantage to owner-training is that service dog coaches often have more time working directly with the owner than traditional program trainers have with a service dog recipient. This extra time allows for ongoing practice and review.

Owner-trainers need to be prepared to respond to business owners and members of the public about their service dog. Some owner-trainers carry copies of legal information, cards or brochures with basic information on service animals. People tend to talk to service dog handlers, and sometimes people may behave in ways that are inappropriate toward the dog. People may even try to distract the service dog. Setting up role-play rehearsal opportunities with clients so they can practice can be very helpful.

Owners also need to know how to react if their dog behaves in a way they did not expect. What if the dog barks? What if the dog acts sick? Service dogs must of course not bark, must be house trained and must never soil or urinate in a store or other inappropriate location. However, sometimes the unexpected happens. Does the owner know what to do? Owners need to know that they should always carry clean-up supplies, and if an accident occurs, clean up (if they are able) and immediately leave. If the dog is sick, the owner needs to take the dog to a veterinarian and keep the dog home until they are fully recovered. Owners need to know that if the dog has a lapse in training or if the dog shows an unexpected behavior, they should discontinue working the dog in public access and reach out to you for guidance. Do not assume that owners know what to do in these various circumstances. Take the time to discuss "what if" situations with the owner.

Owners also need to be educated on the importance of having a back-up plan if their dog is unwell. How will they accommodate their needs if the service dog needs to stay home? People with disabilities who are partnered with service dogs will sometimes state that no, there is no other accommodation. In reality there is almost always an alternative, even if it is far less than ideal. If my power-wheelchair breaks, I can use my manual wheelchair and be pushed by a helper, or I may be able to use my walker and limit the distance I travel. Both of these options are far less than ideal, but they are still viable workarounds. A plan for when the service dog cannot work is essential. Dogs can get sick or injured, or simply need time off.

Etiquette education for service dog clients

Just as the service dog needs to be "invisible," service dog handlers should use appropriate etiquette. Clients need to learn how to give cues softly, and how to redirect their dog's behavior quickly and subtly. Of course, the owner absolutely should praise the dog, but this should not be done loudly when in a no-pets-allowed location. The owner's handling, praise and cues should not draw attention.

While the use of treats should be reduced over time, it is easier for owners to maintain the dog's behavior if they continue to use food rewards intermittently even after the dog is no longer "in training." Context matters. In a restaurant it is not appropriate to reward the dog with food. Consider the location. Food rewards should not be dropped or tossed in buildings. Loud clickers are also inappropriate when working indoors. The team's training should not draw attention.

Training "sneaky cues" can be helpful. These are subtle cues that sound more like conversation. For example, "thank you" can be a cue for attention, or "excuse me" can serve as a cue for the dog to get closer to the owner's side. Using a conversational tone when working with the dog can help train the dog to respond to speech that sounds more like talking and less like training. Working this way helps teams be more discreet in public and can affect how the public responds to the service dog.

Clients need to be prepared to encounter another service dog team. Ideally service dogs do not have any reaction to the presence of another dog and can work in close proximity with another service dog. In the real world, however, it is best for teams to give other service dogs a lot of space.

Field trip training

You think you have covered everything and then suddenly, somehow, a client completely misunderstands your recommendations and does the one thing you absolutely never imagined they would do. Yes, that can happen when you work with owner-trainers and their service dogs, just like it can happen when you work with pet owners. You recommended brief visits to low-key, pet-friendly locations, and the owner takes the dog to a crowded festival for an entire afternoon. While it is obvious to a dog trainer that a festival is a difficult environment for a dog, it may not be to an owner. Public access field trips are not only necessary to train and assess the dog, but also to educate the owner and assess their skills. These are opportunities for service dog coaches to directly show clients what makes a situation challenging for a dog.

As previously discussed, there are advantages to the owner's starting public access training in pets-allowed locations. There are also advantages for the dog. Young dogs can build confidence in environments if they are able to sniff and explore. It's inappropriate for service dogs in training to do that in locations where pets are prohibited. If the dog makes a mistake or sniffs and explores a pet-friendly location, it is usually not a problem.

As when working with pet dog clients, start with the basics and do not make assumptions. Owner-trainers need to be educated on the importance of appropriately sized and fitted training equipment. Leashes, collars, vests and harnesses need to be clean and in good condition. The dog should wear identification tags and any required license tags. The dog should be clean and well-groomed. The owner should have a few basics readily available, including a small-size portable water bowl, treats, a few paper towels and pick-up bags.

Priorities when working with owner-trainers in public locations include the safety of the team and the public, as well as respect for businesses and property. Ensure that your client and the dog are appropriately prepared. Visit field trip locations in advance with your client's needs in mind. Look for accessible parking and curb cuts, as well as appropriate dog relief areas. Prepare clients for the possibility that the field trip may be cut short if the dog is stressed and needs a break.

For people with disabilities, simply exiting a vehicle or negotiating a parking lot can be risky. Clients with sensory disabilities can miss critical information like car horns, blinkers and turn signals. People who use wheelchairs and scooters are harder for drivers to see. Also, the process of opening a wheelchair van and unloading the chair provides a long period of time where the dog can jump out of the vehicle. Have helpers available and then practice basics like unloading the dog from the car in a safe location first, such as a closed private garage.

Begin field trips with easy and brief excursions to stores and shops that allow pets but are not typical locations that people visit with their dogs. I call these "in and out" training sessions. The team enters the shop and then turns around and leaves without even walking through the store. This helps dogs learn how to enter and exit new locations calmly.

From the "in and out" practices, slowly increase the duration and complexity of the outings. As with other training, the process does not follow a straight trajectory. Rather, the training process is always being tweaked in response to the dog's readiness. As the dog gains confidence, ask the dog to perform a few easy skills like Sits and Downs near the entrance before leaving. When the dog improves, the "in and out" turns into a brief walk around the store. Then, when the team gains confidence and skills, the owner purchases a small item.

As the team progresses, additional locations are added to the field trips and the practice sessions become longer and more complex. As a trainer, you are assessing both the dog and the owner's ability to interpret and respond to the dog's needs. Start to introduce no-pets-allowed locations (if permitted by laws in your state) when you are confident in the owner's handling skills, the dog's training and the dog's behavior. The dog should be clearly identified as a service dog in training with a vest or harness.

Locations without a fast exit are the next step. These locations can include shopping malls, larger stores, office buildings and museums. Restaurants and supermarkets are also more difficult because of the proximity of food items. Be considerate of business owners and shoppers, and make sure the dog does not come in contact with food items. Medical facilities, doctor appointments and school campuses may also need to be practiced. Consider real-world challenges encountered in these different locations. Will the dog respond to the owner's cues if the owner is lying down on an exam table?

Other locations where a fast exit is impossible, such as buses, trains and air travel are typically the most difficult. Field trips to these types of locations should be taken when the team is very advanced in their training. Set up clients and their service dogs in training to succeed.

Last but not least, people with disabilities may require emergency medical services. A visit to the community fire station or police station is an opportunity to both train the service dog and educate the emergency personnel about the presence of a service dog in the neighborhood. Check first and make sure that the facility would welcome the team's practice visit.

Elevators and escalators

Elevators and escalators are potentially hazardous for service dogs and service dogs in training. For people with mobility impairments or sensory limitations, just entering and exiting an elevator can be difficult even without a dog. Having a helper secure the elevator door during training practice is important. In most cases, both the dog and owner should enter simultaneously, with the owner closer to the elevator door to prevent it from fully closing.

Whether or not to train service dogs to negotiate escalators is a topic of debate among service dog trainers. I fall on the side of teaching owners to use the elevator instead and avoiding escalators. Even a well-trained service dog could be injured on an escalator if a pass-ersby pushed past the dog. An escalator injury is not only traumatic for the dog, but potentially career ending.

*Exiting elevators can be tricky. The dog needs to
wait for the owner's cue before exiting.*

Transportation

Many people with disabilities rely on public transportation. Wheel-chair accessible transportation may require that the service dog enter using a ramp or a lift, or that the dog be handled by a person other than the dog's owner in order to enter the vehicle. Whenever possible, different options should be practiced.

It can be difficult to prepare a service dog in training for air travel via a true practice situation. Short visits to an airport and trips on a train are reasonable starting points. Practice security screenings. Prepare your client and the dog for security personnel who are nervous about dogs, so the team is ready. The client needs to be able to maintain control even if the dog is directly handled by a stranger and even if the dog's harness or vest is removed. Solid responses to cues like Stand and Stay are essential. Given the high possibility of encountering other service animals, pets and working dogs in air travel, service dogs need to be trained to ignore reactive and aggressive behavior in other animals. Clients need to be taught how to advocate for their dogs and how to make space in difficult situations.

Other public environments and considerations

Because service dogs can go anywhere the public is permitted, there is an endless array of possible environments a dog may need to be prepared to work in, everything from movie theaters and concerts to amusement parks and zoos. Some of the more frequently encountered environments are discussed below.

Wherever the service dog is asked to go, always consider the dog's perspective. Just because the law allows it does not automatically mean a service dog should be taken to a particular environment. There are some environments that would make any dog miserable and anxious. If dogs are repeatedly stressed, over time it will take a toll on their behavioral health and possibly even their physical health. The stress will, eventually, affect a dog's performance as a service dog as well.

Medical appointments and hospitalizations

Medical appointments, dental appointments and hospital stays also require planning and training. Hospital staff cannot be expected to take care of the service dog's needs. Owners need to weigh the logistical challenges of having their dog with them during a hospital stay or medical procedure, and the potential stress on the dog, against the benefits of having the dog with them. How will the dog's needs be met? Can a friend or family member accompany the owner to help handle the dog? For longer hospital stays, it may be more practical for a friend to arrange for visits by the service dog rather than having the dog stay in the hospital with the owner.

When the owner has outpatient medical appointments or dental appointments, service dogs will need to be trained to perform a very solid and long Down-Stay. In some cases, it may be particularly beneficial to bring the service dog. For rehabilitation appointments or for appointments with a mental health provider, it may be helpful for the owner to discuss and even show how the service dog is helping, for example.

The workplace

Clients who wish to bring their service dog to work need to research and prepare themselves with information on how their employer handles disability accommodations. An excellent resource on the ADA and workplace accommodations is the Job Accommodation Network, which can be found online at askjan.org.

Work environments vary greatly. In some cases, the environment may be a very relaxed and low-key setting for the dog. In other cases, the setting may be very demanding. Service dog coaches help clients plan and think about how they will meet the dog's needs at work. Owner-trainers need to be prepared for questions, as well as the possibility of encountering co-workers who dislike dogs or have allergies. Some employers may be very supportive of the service dog while others may not be. The letter of the law is one thing, but the reality of having a pleasant workplace is another.

Schools and colleges

More and more service dogs are working in these settings. Schools and college environments pose significant challenges for the dog, as well as the owner. Young people working with their service dogs in these settings need extra guidance and ongoing support to ensure that they are correctly assessing their dog's stress, giving the dog enough downtime, providing for the dog's behavioral welfare needs and maintaining training appropriately.

Reducing service dogs' stress in public areas

Owner-trainers need to learn how to identify environmental stressors and understand the impact of repeated stressors on an animal's behavioral health. Failing to meet the dog's behavioral needs can have the dramatic effect of shortening the dog's career. Public access field trip lessons are ideal opportunities for owners to learn how to identify their dog's stress and how to respond appropriately. Owner-trainers need education on their dog's stress signs and how to identify when their dog needs a break. Environmental enrichment strategies like food-fillable toys, play, sniff-and-explore walks, calming music and massage should be incorporated into the service dog's care routines. Teach owner-trainers how to include downtime as part of the dog's daily routine to prevent behavior problems and burnout.

Trainers are used to educating owners on signs of stress such as yawning, shaking off, refusing food treats and panting. However, many times the dogs chosen for service work will inhibit their signals. Some dogs will simply do nothing, not engage and seem sullen. Other times the dog appears less enthusiastic, is not playful or is slow to respond to cues. Owners need to be educated on these subtle indicators of stress.

Public access testing and graduating teams

In the beginning of this book, we reviewed a number of differences between service dog coaching and a traditional service dog program. The relationship between a pet dog trainer and an owner-trainer is very different from the relationship between a traditional service dog training program and a service dog recipient. The pet dog trainer offering service dog coaching provides information, training support and guidance. A traditional service dog program provides a finished, task-trained service dog. As a result, one key difference between these models is how teams "graduate" into public access work.

The transition process guided by a service dog coach from in-training status to working status for an owner-trained team is not nearly as dramatic as that of a service dog program, where the service dog recipient has gone to the program to be matched with a service dog. The most obvious difference is that an owner-trainer already owns and lives with the dog. In most cases, the client's dog began performing tasks in the owner's home before public access training was completed. When a service dog coach "graduates" a team, the coach is really just transitioning the team from an intensive training process to training maintenance.

Of course, the role of the service dog coach in providing assessment and evaluation of owner-trained service dog teams is still important. In fact, service dog coaches may use evaluations to help clients identify areas where improvement is needed. Evaluations and observations are a valuable way for the coach to help clients set training goals and document their progress.

The term "graduate" makes it sound like service dogs need to be evaluated only once. One-time evaluations of any type have very limited value. We can all think of pet dogs who passed a test once but would not have passed the same test on a different date. Service dogs need to perform reliably over a period of years. Service dog coaches can evaluate teams multiple times in a wide variety of locations over a period of months. You can create rubrics or checklists with specific training and handling objectives for your clients. Evaluate the dog's actual trained response, the dog's stress levels and the client's handling skills.

Graduation from a traditional service dog program

In the service dog world, traditional programs often use the term "graduate" when referring to teams successfully completing the program's public access test, or PAT. You'll recall that, in this model, applicants interested in a service dog go to the program's location, where they are matched with an already-trained service dog and then educated on how to care for and work with their new dog. The programs' trainers evaluate a team's readiness to work in places pets are not permitted by administering a PAT. There are many different PATs. After the service dog and partner pass the PAT, there is often a graduation ceremony. Reputable programs provide for long-term follow-up to ensure the training is maintained and to support teams in case there are problems.

Service dog coaches may conduct evaluations of teams' work in various real-world environments. For example, assess a team in a restaurant, a store, a supermarket, a parking lot and an office building. Situations like elevators, crowds, entering and exiting vehicles, and encounters with other dogs, other animals and people of different ages are all important to evaluate. Unique environments such as public transportation, buildings that are novel to the team and medical facilities are also good locations. Consider real-world situations where the client needs the dog to work.

The evaluations should also include the dog's response to cues for basic skills and tasks with real-world distractions. Look for indications that the dog is relaxed, confident and responsive to the owner.

How promptly does the dog respond to cues for basic obedience and tasks? Is the dog able to ignore other animals, walk on a loose leash, and enter and exit buildings, elevators and public transportation calmly? How does the team handle small, cramped locations? A one-time assessment gives only a snapshot in time, whereas repeated observations give the trainer a much more accurate picture.

Equally importantly, assessment is an opportunity for you to evaluate your client's skills. Does your client deliver cues and praise in an appropriate tone and discreet way? Is your client providing excellent daily care of the dog? Does your client know how and when to reward the dog? Can your client get the dog's attention when the dog is distracted? Can your client correctly identify when the dog is stressed? Does your client know how to address and prevent stress in the dog? Does your client know how to respond to questions and concerns from business owners and other people? Is the dog's equipment and grooming maintained appropriately? Does your client exhibit appropriate service dog handling etiquette?

You can use video for assessment and to help clients revisit how they and their dog performed, see their strengths and identify areas where additional work is needed. Video can also be a valuable tool for documentation. Service dog coaches are ready to transition their clients to a maintenance plan when both the dogs and owners are sufficiently prepared. The dogs should be regularly working appropriately and confidently, and performing tasks in a relaxed and responsive manner in all types of settings. The owners should be able to demonstrate that they can handle the dog appropriately and responsibly in various public access situations without direct support from the trainer.

9

Accommodating People
with Disabilities in Training

A man who was facilitating a rally obedience match approached me. "We have another one of your people who comes here," he stated. "What?" I was sure I had misheard him. He repeated himself, "We have another of your people who trains here, a person who uses a wheelchair like you." "Ah," I said, trying hard not to laugh at the inappropriateness of his communication.

Although my reaction was to laugh, this situation was, in reality, sad. This person was trying to make me feel welcome, but he had absolutely no idea how completely inappropriate his comment was. Sadly, people with disabilities are still excluded from full participation in society, and some people have, as a result, limited opportunities to interact with people with disabilities.

Communicating with people with disabilities

The term "disability" encompasses a huge and diverse range of human experiences. My reaction to this person's inappropriate remark was to laugh, but others might have felt hurt or angry. One person's experiences with disability can be completely different from another's. It is important to remember that a disability does not fundamentally change who a person is. People with disabilities are simply people.

The man at the rally match assumed that I had a lot in common with another person who used a wheelchair. In fact, people use wheelchairs for many different reasons. One person in a wheelchair may be able to stand and walk short distances while another may be completely paralyzed and have no ability to move or feel their limbs. Some people who use wheelchairs are athletes. Even the wheelchairs themselves can vary greatly. A power wheelchair and a manual wheelchair are vastly different pieces of equipment. This is true for all kinds of disabilities. Two people with the exact same diagnosis may be affected in very different ways.

You may have noticed my use of the phrase "people with disabilities" instead of the terms "handicapped" or "physically challenged." This is referred to as "people first language." People first language is exactly as it is described: The person is referred to first and the condition is described in an objective way. Using people first language, you would say "a person who uses a wheelchair" or "a person with epilepsy," rather than "a wheelchair-bound person" or "an epileptic."

Interactions when talking to a person with a disability are not that different from talking with someone without a disability. Just as when communicating with a person without a disability, make eye contact, smile and ask questions directly to the individual. Allow for extra time and avoid interrupting when communicating with people with disabilities that affect their speech. If you are not sure, it is appropriate to repeat to check for understanding. For instance, "You are asking about whether house training is covered in the class, correct?" Do not pretend you understood when you did not. Paper and pencil or even text messaging can be used to facilitate communication with someone who is deaf or hard of hearing.

It is polite to sit when talking with someone using a wheelchair when possible, so you are both at eye level. Adaptive equipment like canes, walkers and wheelchairs should be treated more like clothing than furniture. Do not lean on or move a wheelchair, walker or other adaptive equipment without asking for permission first.

Some people with disabilities prefer to do things themselves even if they need more time. Ask if help is needed rather than jumping in. Also, be sure to respect clients' need for privacy. If you are working in a training facility, conversations about the client's service dog task training needs should be held in a private room or conducted in a private lesson at the client's home. Last but not least, allow a space in training lesson registration forms for students to share information about accommodations they might need.

Accessibility of training lessons

Examine the training space. Is it accessible and in compliance with the ADA? Be ready to give information about barriers to access. Look at the parking lot. Are there accessible parking spaces and curb cuts? Is the door wide enough? How easily does the door open? What about bathrooms? Check the lighting. For people with limited vision and also for people who are deaf or hard of hearing, additional lighting can facilitate learning. Consider the acoustics of the facility. Are there parts of the training space where it is easier or harder to hear the instructor? Check the floor for trip hazards, and provide chairs for students whose disabilities cause fatigue. Sometimes simple changes like setting up a tether area or moving seating can make a big difference.

Accommodating training techniques

Focusing on owners' strengths rather than their limitations is the key when looking for training solutions that will work for owners and their dogs. For instance, when troubleshooting the use of a clicker by a client with quadriplegia, consider what they can move best. Maybe it's a hand, wrist, thumb or even a foot. Alternatively, perhaps the owner can mark the behavior verbally instead. As much as possible, include the person with the disability in the training process. A person with dementia may be able to deliver a treat after a caregiver clicks. This will allow the person to develop a stronger relationship with the dog, and it is often an empowering experience for the individual.

Common clicker training techniques and strategies can minimize the physical demands of dog training and make it easier for a person with a disability to train their own dog. Compared to other techniques like luring and prompting, free shaping reduces the need for the person to move when training a new behavior. To free shape a new behavior, the trainer marks a behavior the dog offers voluntarily. As the dog offers behaviors that more closely approximate the trainer's goal, the trainer starts to differentially mark and reward those behaviors. For example, if training a service dog candidate to lie down on a mat, initially any movement toward the mat is marked and rewarded. After some practice, the trainer increases the criteria and only clicks and rewards when the dog's front feet touch the mat. Eventually the trainer is only clicking and rewarding when the dog has all four feet on the mat, and lastly when the dog lies down on the mat. Throughout this process, the trainer hardly needs to move. In fact, it is helpful for the trainer to stay in place and let the dog return to receive the reward, so the dog is "reset" for each repetition.

As discussed in Chapter 7, target training can be helpful for clients who have mobility impairments or who use adaptive equipment. However, these clients may not be able to teach the behavior using their hands in the manner described. If a client with a toy breed dog has difficulty bending to complete the early steps of the training process, teaching the dog to touch the end of a target stick instead of a hand can help the client be successful with this important behavior.

Timing and duration of practice lessons also may be affected by training accommodations. Behaviors may need to be broken down more incrementally. Training sessions can be shortened or paced with breaks to accommodate handlers who get tired more quickly.

Training tools

There are many training tools that can be helpful in working with people with disabilities. Hands-free leashes are a good choice for some handlers. However, a hands-free leash may not be safe for someone who is unstable or frail.

Consider the owner's abilities and safety in your training tool choices and accommodations. Choose equipment that gives the owner control without causing the dog pain, stress or discomfort. Also think about how the owner will put the equipment on the dog. For some people, using clasps and buckles can be difficult. Usually larger-sized clasps are easier for people who have limited dexterity.

Clickers with raised buttons are generally easier to use for people with disabilities that affect their hands. For people who use wheelchairs or scooters, the clicker can be affixed to the arm rest to allow the individual to use their wrist or palm to press the clicker. Other options include a verbal marker like "Yes," or making a click sound with the tongue. Use of a target stick can help reduce the need for a person to bend and reach when training the dog.

Delivering treats may also require some creativity. Handlers who use manual wheelchairs or walkers need both hands on their adaptive equipment. Some disabilities affect hand strength and coordination. Large-sized treat bags are usually easier for owner-trainers who have disabilities that affect the use of their hands. Different types of containers to hold treats can often be fastened to a wheelchair or scooter. Owners may find some sizes and textures of treats easier to grab than others. Squeezable plastic tubes can be filled with soft dog food for the dog to lick. They can even be affixed to a wheelchair arm rest. Another option is to reward the dog by offering a lick of peanut butter or canned dog food on a long-handled spoon. Treats can also be tossed rather than handed directly to the dog when working in a dog training facility or outdoors.

Technology may help as well. Training tools like the Pet Tutor can enable owners to participate in the training process. The Pet Tutor can be mounted in different locations, possibly even on some wheelchairs, to facilitate training.

A word of caution before attaching training tools to adaptive equipment. You may inadvertently alter how the equipment works, affect the safety of the equipment or limit the equipment in some way. Attaching items to wheelchairs can add to the width of the chair, making it harder or even impossible for the wheelchair to be used in narrow environments. Anything you add to adaptive equipment to facilitate training the dog should be easily removable. If there is any possibility it could affect the use of the equipment in any way, a rehabilitation specialist should be consulted. In most cases it is not safe to attach a dog's leash directly to adaptive equipment.

For students who have vision impairments, consider noisy dog tags and bright collars. The use of a harness may give the handler more information about the dog's movements than a leash clipped directly to the dog's collar.

Always remember that clients' understanding of training concepts is ultimately much more important than their limitations when it comes to how quickly and effectively they can train their dog. My favorite tool to help clients improve their techniques is video. With an inexpensive cell phone tripod, students can video themselves training their own dog. This allows students to give themselves feedback on timing and technique to see what is working and what is not. Video can also help clients who have disabilities that impact their cognition and learning. The video can help students remember how to practice with their dogs between training appointments. I educate my clients to constructively critique videos of themselves training by watching their video four times as follows:

1. Look at your hair and outfit. OK, now that that is out of the way, you are ready to critique your training.

2. Look at the dog. How is the dog responding to your cues?

3. Look at yourself. How is your technique?

4. Look at yourselves as a team. Is the dog happy? How are you interacting with your dog?

Instructional strategies

Instructional strategies may need to be tweaked to better accommodate people with disabilities. Accommodations for learners with disabilities often have the added benefit of facilitating learning for all students. In most cases only minor changes are needed. Keep in mind that group training is not the right fit for all individuals with disabilities. Be prepared to offer alternative options such as semi-private classes or private lessons.

When you are delivering instruction, speak at a relaxed, normal rate of speed. Use meaningful gestures to support understanding. When demonstrating with a dog, dog trainers tend to look down at the dog and speak at the same time. This makes lip-reading impossible for students who are deaf or hard of hearing! Instead, first describe what you will do while looking at the class. Next demonstrate with the dog. Feel free to describe what you are doing while you demonstrate, but be aware that you will need to repeat this information for students who rely on lip-reading. After your demonstration, review what you did again verbally. A white board, email and handouts can facilitate understanding. Also, be aware that students with visual impairments may have missed important information in your demonstration. Repeating what happened, including stating what the dog did, is important: "I moved the treat upward above Rover's head and Rover sat down."

The seating location in group training classes can also make it easier or more difficult for students with disabilities. For most people with disabilities, sitting closer to the instructor is better than farther away. However, there are exceptions. Students who have mental illness, who are easily fatigued, or who may need a break during the class might be more comfortable when they are closer to an exit.

For some people with disabilities, things take longer to do. Pace the content you cover accordingly when planning training lessons and homework.

Reducing risk

Safety is always a concern when working with people with disabilities and animals. For students with severe limitations of any kind, a caregiver or other helper may be needed. Volunteers in the community and apprentice trainers may also be able and willing to assist.

Students using wheelchairs, walkers and scooters should lock their equipment when they are seated. Providing chairs can help students who have balance issues, or those who are frail or unstable, to train more safely. Be aware. Leashes can get entangled in equipment, which can be dangerous for the dog and owner. Finding just the right length can be tricky. Leashes should not be so long that they drag and get caught on wheels.

When working with a student who uses adaptive equipment, it is usually safer to work without the leash in a safely enclosed space at first. Alternatives include recruiting a helper to hold the dog's leash while the student trains the dog or using a second leash, secured by a helper, as a backup.

Sometimes training accommodations are just not realistic, safe or doable. Board and train or day training can be essential in situations like this. Be careful to replicate working with the dog the same way the owner will in order to facilitate transferring skills. So, for instance, if the owner walks slowly, you need to try to match the owner's pace and gait when training the dog.

10

Long-Term
Training Support

We can all think of pet dog training clients who worked beautifully in puppy class and then disappeared for six months. When they reappear, everything has fallen apart. Ongoing practice helps all dogs maintain their training skills, and it is imperative for service dogs.

Training and coaching support for the owner-trainer over time can be accomplished in a variety of ways. For some teams, group training classes may be appropriate, while for others private lessons are a better fit. Sometimes a combination approach may be helpful. Email, phone or other remote follow-up methods can help keep the communication lines open. As technology continues to expand our options, videoconferencing or similar technology can facilitate providing long-term training support. Trainers who have enough service dog teams may wish to periodically schedule group workshops or public access field trips to keep all of their teams working well.

The frequency of follow-up in part depends on the individual team's needs. For some, annual reassessment combined with email or phone appointments may be sufficient. An at-home-only service dog team is likely to need much less support than a team that is working regularly in public settings. A team where the individual's disability is changing may need more frequent lessons periodically to add tasks.

Some type of reassessment of task training and public access work is always a good idea at least annually, if not more frequently.

Teams also need extra support when the dog's retirement is near. A service dog's retirement is often a challenging time for owner-trainers. It can be helpful to prepare owners for this inevitable reality in advance. Most service dogs will need to retire between the ages of 8 and 10 years old. Some dogs may be able to continue to perform tasks at home for longer, while others may need to retire sooner if they develop a medical or behavioral issue. Dogs who perform physically demanding tasks such as brace and balance tasks or wheelchair pulling usually have to retire sooner. Again, this can be customized according to the individual situation and need. In some cases, a service dog may be able to continue working with a lighter workload. For example, the dog may be able to work fewer public access hours and retire gradually.

The vast majority of owner-trainers will choose to keep their dog after the dog needs to retire. Occasionally it may not be in the dog's best interest. For instance, if the owner-trainer needs to get another service dog and the older, retired dog would be stressed by the change, rehoming might be the better option. By having conversations about plans for the dog's retirement early, service dog coaches can encourage owners to make sure that their dogs' needs are met.

11

Are You Ready?

Starting to offer a new specialty training service can be intimidating. It is hard to know if you are truly ready. While service dog coaching is an exciting area of work that is in high demand, it can get complicated very quickly. Before jumping in, it is a good idea to evaluate if you and your business are ready to start offering service dog coaching.

Self-assess your skills, experience and knowledge

1. Are you familiar with the federal, state and local laws in your area regarding service dogs and service dog training?

2. Do you have a strong foundation of experience training basic skills using positive reinforcement to a variety of dogs of many different breeds?

3. Do you know how to train complex service dog tasks using clicker training and other positive reinforcement techniques?

4. Do you have experience conducting behavior evaluations? Do you know how to evaluate a potential service dog candidate?

5. Are you knowledgeable about working with people with disabilities? Do you know how to adapt training so people with

disabilities can safely participate in the training process? Are you prepared to respect client confidentiality?

6. Do you have the knowledge and skills to prepare dogs for public access work and to assess a team's readiness to work independently in public access?

7. Do you know how to work collaboratively with healthcare providers to help people with disabilities determine appropriate tasks for their service dog?

8. Do you have strong people skills? Are you comfortable helping people set realistic expectations and understand accurate information about their dogs?

Is your business ready?

1. Is your business legal structure and insurance appropriate for service dog training?

2. Do you have contracts, medical releases and paperwork necessary for service dog training support, all reviewed by an attorney?

3. Do you have an ADA-accessible facility? Does your training space allow for the privacy that may be needed for task training? Alternatively, are you able to work with owners in their homes and other accessible locations?

4. Is your staff educated about how to communicate and work with people with disabilities? Is your staff able to maintain appropriate client confidentiality?

5. Do you have a customizable process ready for intake, evaluation and service dog training client education?

Just as there are aggression cases that are far more complex and difficult than others, some service dog situations are more challenging than others. Ethical trainers are prepared to refer clients they do not feel qualified to help to trainers who are. In most cases, an at-home-only service dog is much easier to train than a full public access service dog. However, as discussed previously, it is always important to make sure the owner is on the same page and in agreement that the dog is being trained for at-home-only service work.

Opportunities to learn more

There are growing opportunities for trainers to gain education and experience in service dog work. From webinars to courses and workshops, there are many options available for professionals interested in this field. *Cooperative Paws Service Dog Coach* is the certification program I founded to prepare pet dog trainers to train service dogs and support owner-trainers. This program covers knowledge, skills and task training, and includes service dog training business tools. Professional organizations like the Association of Professional Dog Trainers, the Pet Professional Guild and the International Association of Animal Behavior Consultants also offer webinars and articles about service dog training. The Resources section of this book includes a number of educational organizations, educational programs, books and websites.

Local service dog programs are another wonderful opportunity to learn and gain some hands-on experience. Service dog programs often look for volunteers. Because this is an unregulated industry, trainers need to do their homework and research carefully before volunteering, to make sure they are learning from a quality program. Although therapy dog work is not the same thing as service dog work, there are some commonalities. In both cases, the focus is on human-animal interaction. Assisting in therapy dog program evaluations can provide trainers experience in evaluating dogs, as well as skills in communicating with their owners about the results of the evaluations.

Gaining understanding and experience with people with disabilities is an important and often overlooked aspect of working with service dogs. Community organizations for people with disabilities, hospitals and rehabilitation facilities may need volunteers. Spending time working with people with disabilities is invaluable for a future service dog coach.

Final considerations

Much of the emphasis in the service dog world has been on how to train service dogs to better help people. As the role of service dogs continues to expand, more and more dogs are being trained to participate in various aspects of service work. While there are wonderful service dog programs and a growing appreciation for the value of human-animal interactions, there are also abuses in the service dog industry. There are, sadly, service dog programs and trainers who do not use gentle, positive methods, and who disregard a dog's welfare.

As we consider the question of how to mitigate the damage these unscrupulous programs can cause, we need to expand our focus to address the question: How can we teach people to better help service dogs? We need to make sure we are making realistic demands and balancing humans' needs with dogs' needs.

Dogs working as service dogs need daily, unstructured time to move about naturally. It is not fair to expect any dog to work constantly. Environmental enrichment, sufficient sleep, and play are important for a wonderful quality of life for pet dogs and are equally essential for service dogs. Ultimately this is a win-win. Giving service dogs what they need to be relaxed and happy allows them to be at their best when they support their owners.

Pet dog trainers are uniquely positioned to support and advocate for the needs of service dogs. By offering service dog coaching, pet dog trainers can educate owners on how to provide for their service dogs, how to understand their service dogs' needs and how to identify their dogs' limitations. Pet dog training professionals can promote high-quality training and care of service dogs and support people with disabilities in their communities.

My garden was beautiful in spite of the hot summer day. I did not realize how the heat was affecting me. Suddenly, I stumbled and awkwardly realized I could not get back up from the ground. Initially I was embarrassed, thinking maybe someone saw me, but no one was around. I had a sinking feeling as I realized no one would find me for at least six more hours. Monty, my shepherd mix, rushed toward me. He stood next to me patiently, and with his support, I was able to stand. We slowly walked back to the house together.

Resources

Suggested reading

Dog training and behavior foundations

Clicking with Your Dog: Step-by-Step in Pictures, 2000, Peggy Tillman. Information on getting started implementing clicker training.

The Human Half of Dog Training, Collaborating with Clients to Get Results, 2012, Risë Van Fleet. Practical strategies to communicate with dog owners effectively.

On Talking Terms with Dogs: Calming Signals, 2006, Turid Rugaas. Classic book on dog body language and identifying stress.

The Other End of the Leash, 2003, Patricia McConnell. Book on human-animal interaction and understanding strategies to improve communication with dogs.

The Power of Positive Training, 2008, Pat Miller. Information on how to implement positive training techniques and understand dog body language.

Service dog books

Lend Me an Ear: Temperament, Selection and Training of the Hearing Ear Dog, 2013, Martha Hoffman. How to assess and train a hearing alert dog.

Healing Companions: Ordinary Dogs and Their Extraordinary Power to Transform Lives, 2010, Jane Miller. Information on service dogs for people with mental illness.

Training Your Diabetic Alert Dog, 2013, Rita Martinez and Sue Barnes. Information on how to train a diabetic alert dog to alert to blood sugar changes.

Educational programs

CATCH Canine Trainers Academy, www.catchdogtrainers.com. Educational programs in pet dog training including certification and mentorship. Website includes a directory of trainers.

Cooperative Paws Service Dog Coach™, www.cooperativepaws.com. Service dog courses including a certificate program in service dog coaching for pet dog trainers. Website includes a listing of trainers who completed the author's program in service dog coaching.

Karen Pryor Academy, www.karenpryoracademy.com. Educational programs in pet dog training with a focus on clicker training. Website includes a listing of graduates.

Peaceable Paws, peaceablepaws.com. Educational programs in pet dog training, certification program and courses. Website includes trainer referrals and graduates.

The Academy, www.academyfordogtrainers.com. Educational program in dog training and behavior. Website includes a listing of graduates.

Victoria Stilwell Academy for Dog Trainers, www.vsdogtrainingacademy.com. Educational program in pet dog training that includes mentorship. Website includes a listing of graduates.

Organizations

Assistance Dogs International, www.assistancedogsinternational.org. An organization that sets standards for nonprofit service dog programs. Website includes a listing of service dog programs.

The Association of Professional Dog Trainers, www.apdt.com. An organization that promotes education and provides support for professional dog trainers. Website includes a listing of members.

Certification Council for Professional Dog Trainers, www.ccpdt.org. The CCPDT is a certification program for professional pet dog trainers. The website includes a listing of certified pet dog trainers.

International Association of Animal Behavior Consultants, www.iaabc. org. An organization that promotes education and offers support to animal behavior consultants. The organization includes a working animal division and a listing of behavior consultants.

International Association of Assistance Dog Partners, www.iaadp.org. An organization that supports assistance dog partners and includes extensive information about assistance dogs, as well as tasks and training information online.

Pet Professional Guild, www.petprofessionalguild.com. An organization that advocates for force-free training for dogs and supports professional trainers committed to force-free training. The website includes a listing of professional trainers.

Websites

ADA Requirements: Service Animals, www.ada.gov/service_animals_2010.htm. Department of Justice clarification of the definition of service animals.

Frequently Asked Questions about Service Animals and the ADA, www.ada.gov/regs2010/service_animal_qa.html. Department of Justice information about service animals.

HABRI Central: Resources for the Study of the Human-Animal Bond, habricentral.org. Online research and resources on service animals, therapy animal information.

Information and Technical Assistance on the Americans with Disabilities Act, www.ada.gov. Information on the Americans with Disabilities Act including service animal law.

Prescribing Animals for Human Health: Above all do no harm. www. mmilani.com/7270/prescribing-animals-human-health-no-harm. A website with a blog on human-animal interactions including several articles on service dogs, including this one on the complexity of service animal use.

Karen Pryor Clicker Training, www.clickertraining.com A website with many articles and videos on clicker training concepts. An online store also sells clicker training books and supplies.

Products

Pet Tutor, www.smartanimaltraining.com. A remote training tool that can be used in a variety of ways to dispense treats from a distance and can be operated with a smart phone or tablet.

The Puppy Class Curriculum, www.dogbizsuccess.com. A comprehensive puppy class training curriculum with tools including the Puppy Passport.

Service dog leads and harnesses, www.boldleaddesigns.com. Different types of harnesses and leashes including some custom service dog equipment.

Service dog vests, www.raspberryfield.com. A supplier of custom made service dog vests.

About the Author

Veronica Sanchez, M.Ed., CABC, CPDT-KA, is the founder of the *Cooperative Paws Service Dog Coach* certificate program for professional pet dog trainers. Veronica's passion for service dogs is personal and professional. She has over 20 years of experience in professional pet dog training and has supported owners training service dogs for a wide range of needs including psychiatric,  mobility, hearing and even a dual guide-mobility dog. Veronica has a disability herself, a neurological disorder called generalized dystonia, and she trained her own dogs to assist as service dogs.

Veronica has degrees in education and psychology from George Mason University, and a certificate in brain research in education from the University of Washington. She is a Certified Animal Behavior Consultant, a Certified Professional Dog Trainer–Knowledge Assessed and a former vice president of the International Association of Animal Behavior Consultants. Veronica often speaks and writes on service dogs for professional organizations including the Association of Professional Dog Trainers and the Pet Professional Guild.

Veronica, her husband and their canine family live in Vienna, Virginia. Learn more about Veronica and her programs at www.cooperativepaws.com.

Index

Also available from Dogwise Publishing

Go to dogwise.com for more books and ebooks.

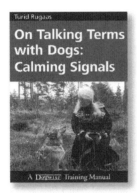

On Talking Terms with Dogs.

Calming Signals, 2nd Ed

Turid Rugaas

Norwegian dog trainer Turid Rugaas taught the world that humans cannot only learn to read canine body language but use their own body language to communicate with dogs. One of the most influential books on dog behavior today.

Right on Target!

Taking Dog Training to a New Level

Mandy Book and Cheryl S. Smith

"Target training" rewards your dog for touching your hand, a target stick or just about any object you choose to help shape the behavior you want. A fun and useful skill for the family dog or dog sport competitor.

Canine Body Language.

A Photographic Guide

Brenda Aloff

Ever wish you could talk to your dog? With this bible of canine body language you can learn to read him! Well-organized, loaded with photos and detailed explanations, it helps you interpret your dog's emotions and, indeed, thoughts.

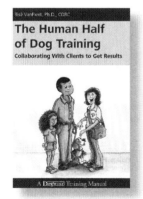

The Human Half of Dog Training

Collaborating with Clients to Get Results

Risë VanFleet, PhD, CDBC

Dog trainers don't really train dogs—they train people to train their dogs. Learn how to empathize with clients, overcome common objections and work with families to get the best results for the dog. From a PhD Psychologist-turned-dog-trainer.

Dogwise.com is your source for quality books, eBooks, DVDs and VOD.

We've been selling to the dog fancier for more than 30 years and we carefully screen our products for quality information. You'll find something for every level of dog enthusiast on our website Dogwise.com or drop by out store in Wenatchee, Washington.

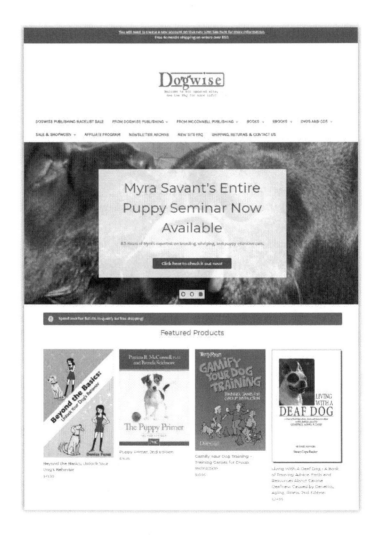

Made in the USA
Middletown, DE
28 February 2019